A First Stamp Album
FOR BEGINNERS

ROBERT OBOJSKI

Dover Publications, Inc.
New York

Published in Canada by General Publishing Company, Ltd., 30 Lesmill Road, Don Mills, Toronto, Ontario.
Published in the United Kingdom by Constable and Company, Ltd.

A First Stamp Album for Beginners is a new work, first published by Dover Publications, Inc., in 1984.

International Standard Book Number: 0-486-23843-1

Manufactured in the United States of America
Dover Publications, Inc., 31 East 2nd Street, Mineola, N.Y. 11501

Introduction

Welcome to the exciting hobby of stamp collecting! You are now part of a large group of people from all over the world who share a lively interest in the beauty and history of postage stamps. The fact that stamp collecting has long been the most popular hobby in the world, with over 16 million enthusiasts in the United States alone, is a good indication of how much fascination and appeal these colorful little pieces of gummed paper exert. Another is the fact that many collectors are adults who became interested in the hobby when they were children and have found it a stimulating and fun activity throughout their lives. The more they learn about the world of postage stamps, the more enjoyment they get from each new addition to their collection. Each new stamp from a faraway place brings to the collector some of the excitement and adventure of foreign travel, and a curiosity to learn more about that country—where is it, how large is it, how old is it, how many people live there, what languages do its citizens speak, what is life there like, and so forth. No doubt you will quickly fall under the spell of postage stamps yourself, and become a *philatelist*, a fancier word for stamp collector.

The History of Stamp Collecting in a Nutshell

The hobby of stamp collecting began soon after the first adhesive (gummed-back) postage stamp was issued by Great Britain in 1840, almost 150 years ago. Because it cost only one penny and showed a profile portrait of the then twenty-one-year-old Queen Victoria on a black

Figure 1. The first true postage stamp ever issued—the famous Penny Black, which dates from 1840.

background, this now very famous stamp is known as the Penny Black. It's so old, and therefore rare and expensive, you're not very likely to come across one soon, but be on the lookout anyway. Many fabulously rare stamps have been found by amateur collectors purely by chance. In some ways stamp collecting is a little like playing detective!

After Great Britain issued the Penny Black, other countries quickly realized that issuing stamps was a very good way to pay for the costs of running a public postal system. Up until that time, letter delivery systems were mostly in private hands and very expensive—way beyond the means of the average citizen. There was also a good deal of confusion and not a little dishonesty in the earlier systems; sometimes the person sending a letter prepaid the delivery charges, and sometimes letters were sent "collect," meaning that the person receiving it was expected to pay for its delivery. Unfortunately, many clever people quickly learned how to cheat the system; they would put their message in a simple code on the envelope itself, as part of the address, and then send it collect. The person receiving it would glance at the envelope, quickly decipher the code—thereby receiving the message—and then refuse to accept the letter or pay the expensive delivery charges! Cheap postage did away with these abuses of the system and led to fast, efficient mail-delivery systems all over the world.

An indication of the postage stamp's success is that 30 years after the Penny Black was issued a total of over 7,000 different stamps were being issued by many countries. The number of different stamps being issued doubled by the year 1914, and nowadays well over 15,000 different stamps are issued each year by every government in the world. It has been estimated that altogether more than 400,000 different adhesive postal stamps have been issued to date!

With such a vast number of stamps in existence, it is impossible for any one collector to have a complete collection, containing a specimen of every stamp ever issued. Nevertheless some serious philatelists have tried for completeness and have spent enormous fortunes in their search for rare items to fill the empty spaces in their bulging albums. But most collectors eventually find it more interesting to begin to specialize in one or two kinds or varieties of stamps, thereby making it at least within the realm of possibility to form a complete collection. Some concentrate on stamps from a single country; others collect only stamps with pictures of birds on them, or flowers, or famous women, or renowned scientists, or airplanes, or boats. The list of possible topical specialties is endless.

Others decide to limit their collection to stamps of unusual shapes, say diamond or triangular, while others focus on stamps with printing errors (upside down pictures, for instance) or airmail stamps. A particularly interesting special type is the commemorative, a stamp issued to honor a person or to mark the anniversary of an important event.

Another form of specialization would be to limit one's collection to *mint* stamps, stamps that have never seen postal duty and thus have not been cancelled. Cancellation is the process of imprinting black lines over stamps when a letter is processed at the post office, in order to prevent their being used over again. In the early years of stamp production the cancellation process was not perfect, and it was possible for people to "clean" stamps and reuse them over and over, thereby causing great financial problems for the postal systems.

Where to Begin

The stamp album you now have is ideal for beginning collectors. It pictures over 1,100 quite easy-to-find stamps from almost 200 different countries. When you find a stamp that looks like one shown, place it right over the illustration. Double-check, though, to make sure the stamp is an *exact* match to the picture – for instance, that the *denomination* (amount of money the stamp sold for in the post office when it was first issued) is the same. The only differences between the stamps you find and those pictured should be (1) that the actual stamps are printed in colors whereas all the pictures in this album are in black and white, and (2) that the actual stamps are also slightly larger (about 10 per cent) than the pictured ones.

Within the space devoted to the 196 countries (technically called *issuing authorities*) there are also many blank boxes where you can put stamps from that nation which are not pictured. Altogether there are spaces for more than 2,350 stamps in the main part of the album (pages 1–63) and room for 240 more in the extra blank

pages at the end that you can use for whatever purpose you decide is appropriate. Perhaps you'll want to use these pages to begin a specialized collection of your own.

If you are careful to put your stamps in the album in just the way we describe below, you'll be able to remove them easily any time you want and perhaps eventually put them in a larger album picturing every stamp ever issued in the whole world! You'll have to save about $50, though, in order to buy such a complete album.

How to Obtain Stamps Cheaply

One of the nicest things about stamp collecting is that it need not be an expensive hobby. In fact you can get a lot of interesting stamps absolutely free! Just let your relatives, friends and neighbors know that you are starting a collection and you'll find that they will be glad to give you all the stamps they receive on their mail. Even if you get only three or four people to help you, you'll quickly gather a large number of stamps.

Another source of free stamps is other stamp collectors. All collectors accumulate duplicates, extra copies of stamps. After examining all the copies he has of a particular stamp and saving the cleanest and freshest-looking one for his own collection, every collector is eager to trade the others for stamps he does not yet own. Perhaps there is a stamp collecting club at your school; if so, join it and have fun learning about stamps and their history and meet people who will be interested in swapping stamps with you.

Packages of stamps can be purchased at dime stores, department stores and hobby shops. You can get quite a large number of stamps for a dollar or less, but generally the more stamps you get for your money, the lower the quality will be. In other words, the "bargain" packages with lots of stamps in them will tend to have rather worn, very common stamps, and lots of duplicates. Other, slightly more expensive, packages, or packages selling for the same price but containing fewer stamps, will have better quality stamps and fewer duplicates.

Using This Album

In order to use this album, you have to understand how it is organized. Actually it's set up much like almost every other stamp album, even the most complete ones. The countries or issuing authorities are arranged alphabetically according to their names in the English language, except that the United States comes first, followed by the United Nations, and countries that were once territories, colonies or possessions of England, Holland, France or other countries are generally located following the "mother country."

You'll notice that the countries in this album are numbered 1 (United States) through 196 (Yemen Arab Republic). These little numbers that appear just above and to the left of each country's name will be very useful to you; they'll make it possible for you to quickly locate exactly where to place any stamp you may come across!

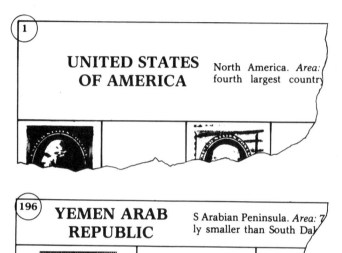

Figure 2. The numbers circled in this illustration are the ones referred to in the Stamp Identifier Table.

We'll give two examples to show how easy it is to decide the right place to put almost any stamp you find, even very "mysterious" ones. Let's suppose you have obtained the two stamps pictured below. The first thing to do is study each one carefully to try to discover what the most prominent word or words on it are. The largest word on the stamp on the left is certainly "Österreich." Turn to the alphabetically arranged Stamp Iden-

Figure 3. Two stamps you can easily identify using the Stamp Identifier Table.

tifier Table (pages viii–x) and look in the O's for Österreich. You'll quickly find it, followed by the number 10. Thumb through the album keeping your eyes on the little numbers above and to the left of the names of the countries until you come to number 10 on page 12. You'll find that the German-speaking country that calls itself Österreich is known in English as Austria!

Now let's look at the stamp on the right. The most prominent words are "Magyar Posta." You'll probably guess that "Posta" means postage, so let's forget it and look up "Magyar" in the Stamp Identifier Table. You'll find that it's number 133, and when you locate that number in the album (page 46), you see it refers to the country known in English as Hungary. This special system of numbers and the Stamp Identifier Table let you identify stamps from all over the world, even stamps issued by countries whose names have changed over the years, without having to know German, Hungarian or any other foreign language.

This is a good time to mention that the only country in the world that doesn't put its name on all its postage is Great Britain. Perhaps this has something to do with the fact that that was the first country to issue postage stamps. But stamps from Great Britain are not hard to identify; indeed, the mere absence of a country's name is your first and best clue to the stamp's being British. Other clues are that British stamps *almost always* (1) include the world words "postage" and "revenue" on them; (2) show a portrait of the king or queen reigning at the time the stamp was issued; and (3) indicate the number of pence the stamp cost by means of the abbreviation "d" (up until the year 1969) or "p." Therefore, if you find a stamp that doesn't seem to have a country's name on it but does carry the words "2d" (twopence) or "4p" (four pence), for example, you can be pretty sure it's from Great Britain.

You'll notice that next to each country's name we've given you some facts about the size of that nation, usually compared to that of one or more of our States; the number of people living there; the language spoken there; the political status (republic, colony, dependency, etc.); the name of the capital city; and the name of the units of currency. This information is given just to whet your appetite; you'll want to learn more about each country whose stamps you encounter, and easy ways of getting additional information are discussed at the end of this introduction.

Another very special feature of this album is that it includes dates of issue for all stamps pictured. Where you see a single year under a picture, it means that that stamp was only issued during that one year. An entry like 1925–1928, on the other hand, means that that stamp was issued over a four-year period. Generally speaking, the longer the period of issue, the more stamps were produced and the less likely they are to be rare. As in most stamp albums, each country's oldest regular issue stamps are shown first and the most recent ones last. Airmail, Special Delivery and other special issues are placed after the regular issues.

The Right Way to Handle and Mount Stamps

Now that you know how this album is arranged and how to identify any stamps that you may find, you're ready to learn the proper way to handle stamps and the correct way to mount them in the album.

Of course, stamp collecting is primarily a hobby that one does for the sheer fun and excitement of it, but there is a monetary or financial aspect to it as well because some stamps are valuable and many are worth at least a few dollars. Any stamp's value is determined partly on the basis of its rarity and partly by its physical condition, so stamp collectors are careful not to damage stamps while handling them. Unfortunately, there have been many cases in which priceless stamps have been rendered worthless by mishandling.

Here are a few important "DO NOTS" to keep firmly in mind:

1. Never cut into a stamp or trim off any part of its perforated edges.

2. Don't separate stamps that are joined together by their original perforations. A block of four stamps, for instance, is often worth more than the same four stamps would be individually.

3. Don't handle stamps any more than you have to. Natural skin oils from your fingers can stain stamps permanently. Most stamp collectors use stamp tongs to handle their stamps. These tongs are very inexpensive and can be purchased in hobby shops and department stores. Never use tweezers; these have sharp points on the ends which will puncture the stamps.

4. Don't leave stamps in direct sunlight for long periods of time. The colors will fade.

Now, here are a few important "DO'S" to remember:

1. There's only one correct way to remove a used postage stamp from an envelope. All other ways will result in damaged stamps.

First, cut off all the envelope except for about a half-inch all around the stamps. Next, soak this piece of envelope with the stamps on it in a clean dish of warm (not hot) water for 15 or 20 minutes, until the glue dissolves and the stamps float off the paper backing. Finally, put the stamps on a piece of blotting paper to prevent them from curling up. Don't touch them again until they are completely dry.

2. Stamp collectors never use paste or tape to mount their stamps because over a period of time these adhesives will seep through the paper and stain the face of the stamps. They also make it impossible to remove stamps from albums without damaging them. You will want to be able to remove stamps easily because you'll constantly be upgrading your collection, removing some specimens and replacing them with ones of better quality.

Always use special transparent stamp hinges to mount stamps in albums. They are very inexpensive, and you can buy packages of them in any dime store, stationery store or hobby shop. When you are ready to mount a stamp, hold one of the hinges with the adhesive side up, fold it back a little ways as shown in the figure, and then lightly moisten the folded-back part.

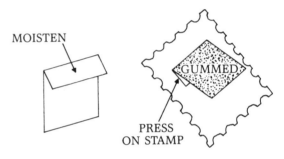

Figure 4. How to mount stamps in an album by means of transparent stamp hinges with gummed backs.

Attach that part of the hinge to the back of the stamp, in the center just below the top perforation. Next lightly moisten the rest of the hinge and affix that part to the album page.

Once the hinge has dried completely you'll be able to detach it from the album and from the stamp easily, without damaging either of them.

Hints on Developing Your New Hobby

Always keep your loose stamps and your stamp album clean and neat. Remember that stamp collecting may turn into a lifelong hobby, lasting years and years. These little pieces of paper we call stamps are fragile and must be treated with care.

The more you learn about stamps and their history, the more enjoyment you will get out of your hobby. When you are working with your stamp collection try to have an atlas, an almanac and perhaps even an encyclopedia nearby, and take the time to find out more about the interesting countries, people, flowers, animals, mountains and other things that stamps will introduce you to. Go to the library and get and read some books on the fascinating hobby of stamp collecting.

You'll also enjoy your hobby much more if you get to know other people who share an interest in stamps. Introduce yourself to the people who run your local hobby shop or stamp-collecting store; they'll be glad to help you and put you in touch with other collectors and perhaps even groups of collectors who meet regularly to talk about the world of postage stamps.

Glossary

We'll close with a short alphabetical list of some special terms stamp collectors use. You'll find that soon you'll be using them too!

Block. An unsevered group of stamps, at least two stamps wide and two stamps high.

Commemorative. A special stamp issued to honor a person or to celebrate an historical event. Commemoratives are usually issued only for short periods of time.

Definitive. A *regular* issue as opposed to a commemorative.

Face value. The original set value of the stamp, its original value for postal purposes.

Gum. The adhesive applied to backs of postage stamps.

Imperforate. A stamp which has no perforations. Most early stamps were imperforate.

Mint stamp. An unused stamp in perfect condition, looking as though it were just purchased at the post office with fresh color, full gum adhesive on the back and all perforations intact.

Pair. Two unsevered stamps.

Pane. An intact sheet of stamps exactly as originally purchased at the post office.

Perforations. Rows of small, usually round holes, placed between the stamps on a sheet so that they can easily be separated. If a stamp has perforations on only one, two or three sides instead of on all four sides, it is known as a *part-perforate*.

Philately. The official, formal word for stamp collecting. Similarly, a stamp collector is called a *philatelist*.

Postage due. A stamp put on a letter or package at the post office when the sender has used insufficient postage. This stamp indicates the amount of money that must be collected by the postman from the person who receives the mail.

Regular issue. The everyday, ordinary kind of stamp, as opposed to an airmail, special delivery, postage due, commemorative or other kind of special purpose stamp.

Watermark. A design or pattern incorporated into the paper upon which postage stamps are printed. Watermarks help to prevent forgeries.

Stamp Identifier Table and Index

This alphabetical list contains the names of all the countries in their own languages as well as in English. It also contains other words found on stamps that will help you identify them. The numbers refer to the small boldface numerals that appear just above and to the left of the names of the countries in the album (see "Using This Album," page iv).

UNITED STATES OF AMERICA

North America. *Area:* 3,618,467 sq. mi. (the fourth largest country in the world). *Pop.:* 236,800,000. *Cap.:* Washington, D.C. *Lang.:* English. *Money:* 100 cents = 1 dollar.

1883	1890–93		1890–93
	1890–93		
		1890–93	
	1893		
1902–3	1902–3	1902–3	
1917–19 · 1917–19 · 1917–19 · 1917–19 · 1917–19			1917–19
1922–34 · 1922–34 · 1922–34	1922–34		

1927

1929

1929

1930

1932

1932

1932

1933

1933

1933

1933

1934

1934

1934

1934

1934

1935

1940

1936

1936

1936–7

1939

1940

1945

1938–54	1938–54	1938–54	1938–54	1938–54	
1938–54	1938–54	1938–54	1938–54	1938–54	
1940	1940	1940	1940	1940	1940
1940		1940		1940	
1947		1948	1958	1960	1960	1960
1940	1940	1942	1942	1943	1943	1946
1952					
1947			1956		1956

1943–44

1945–46

1964–68   1964–68   1964–68   1964–68   1964–68   1964–68

1964–68   1964–68   1964–68   1964–68   1964–68   1964–68

1964–68   1964–68   1964–68   1964–68   1964–68

1966–73

CHAMPION OF LIBERTY

1968   1968   1968–69   1968–69   1959   1959

1959   1959   1960   1960   1960   1960

1960–61   1960–61   1960–61   1960–61

1962   1964   1964   1966   1966

4

1960–66	1962–66	1966

| 1965–73 | 1965–73 | 1965–73 | 1965–73 | 1965–73 | 1965–73 | 1965–73 |

| 1965–73 | 1965–73 | 1965–73 | 1965–73 | 1965–73 | 1965–73 |

| 1966–73 | 1966–73 | 1966–73 | 1967 | 1970 |

| 1970–74 | 1970–74 | 1970–74 | 1970–74 | 1970–74 | 1970–74 |

| 1970–74 | 1969 | 1969 |

| 1971 | 1971 |

| 1975 | 1975 |

1969	1969	1973	1973	1976

1973

1974

1974

1974

1974

1974

1973–74	1973–74	1973–77		1975–77
1975–77	1975–77	1975–77		1975–77
	1975–77	1975–77		1977
1977				

1975			
1975		1975	1975
1976	1976	1976	1976
1975	1976	1976	1977

	USA 13¢	A US Postage	USA 15¢
	1978	1978	1978

Airmails and Special Delivery

AIR 30 MAIL UNITED STATES OF AMERICA		AIR MAIL 5¢ UNITED STATES OF AMERICA	
1941–44		1946	
AIR MAIL	FIFTIETH ANNIVERSARY UNITED STATES AIR FORCE U.S. AIR MAIL POSTAGE 6¢	US AIR MAIL	
1948	1957	1958–60	

1959

1959

1959–60

1961

1968

1971–73

1971–73

1971–73

1944

1957

1971

2 UNITED NATIONS

Association of sovereign states with membership open to all countries of the world which espouse the cause of peace. There are currently 152 nations represented at the U.N. The first United Nations stamps were issued in 1951.

1951

1966

1969

1974

3

CANAL ZONE

Strip of land extending 5 miles on each side of the axis of the Panama Canal under jurisdiction | of the U.S. by treaty with Panama since 1903. *Area:* 553 sq. mi. *Pop.:* 43,000.

| 1924–26 | 1949 | 1958 |

4

HAWAII

Became the 50th state in 1959. Formerly a kingdom and republic, it issued its own stamps from 1851 to 1899.

| 1882 | 1890–91 | 1899 |

5

AFGHANISTAN

Central Asia. *Area:* 260,000 sq. mi. (slightly smaller than Texas). *Pop.:* 14,699,000. *Cap.:* | Kabul. *Langs.:* Pashtu and Persian. *Money:* 100 pouls = 1 rupee Afghani.

| 1931–38 | 1950 |

6

ALBANIA
[Shqiperia]

SE Europe. *Area:* 11,100 sq. mi. (slightly larger than Maryland). *Pop.:* 2,626,000. *Cap.:* Tirana. | *Langs.:* Albanian and Greek. *Money:* 100 quintar = 1 lek.

| 1920 | 1925 |

7

ANDORRA
[Andorre]

SW Europe. *Area:* 180 sq. mi. (half the size of New York City). *Pop.:* 34,000. *Cap.:* Andorra la Vella. *Langs.:* Catalan (off.), French and Spanish. | *Money:* 100 centimes = 1 franc (French currency) and 100 centimos = 1 peseta (Spanish currency).

| 1931 | 1944 | 1945 |

ARGENTINA

South America. *Area:* 1,072,067 sq. mi. (four times the size of Texas). *Pop.:* 27,210,000. *Cap.:* Buenos Aires. *Lang.:* Spanish. *Money:* 100 centavos = 1 peso.

1892–95	1899	1908–09
1915		1920
1930		
1952	1959–70	
1959–70		1968

ALGERIA
[Algérie]

N Africa. Formerly a semi-autonomous département of France. *Area:* 919,591 sq. mi. (more than three times the size of Texas). *Pop.:* 18,145,000. *Cap.:* Algiers. *Langs.:* Arabic, Berber and French. *Money:* 100 centimes = 1 franc; since 1964, 100 centimes = 1 dinar.

1924	1926	1954–56
1937	1942	

AUSTRIA

[Österreich]

Central Europe. In 1876, the Austro-Hungarian Monarchy was established, with Austria and Hungary as equal partners. After World War I the various nationalities of the monarchy established their own states. *Area:* 32,376 sq. mi. (slightly smaller than Maine). *Pop.:* 7,506,000. *Cap.:* Vienna. *Langs.:* German and Slovene. *Money:* 100 Heller = 1 Krone; since 1925, 100 Groschen = 1 Schilling.

1867–72

1896

1906–07

1908

1908

1908

1929

1930

1934

1946–47

1948–49

1951–52

1957–60

1957–60

1966

1925

1926

1926

BOSNIA and HERZEGOVINA

Located SE Europe in what is now Yugoslavia. Provinces of Austria-Hungary from 1908 to 1918.

1912–14

1917

1917

BELGIUM

[Belgique, België]

W Europe. *Area:* 11,779 sq. mi. (slightly larger than Maryland). *Pop.:* 9,849,000. *Cap.:* Brussels.

Off. Langs.: Flemish and French. *Money:* 100 centimes = 1 franc; 5 francs = 1 belga.

1869–70

1886–91

1905–07

1915

1919–20

1921–23

1921–23

1929–30

1931

1938–42

1950

1950–52

1957–60

1958

1960

1961

1961

ZAIRE

[Congo Belge, République Démocratique du Congo]

Central Africa. Former Belgian colony. *Area:* 905,065 sq. mi. (one-fourth the size of the United | States). *Pop.:* 28,090,000. *Cap.:* Kinshasa. *Off. Lang.:* French. *Money:* 100 makuta = 1 zaire.

1925–26

1925–26

1952–53

1965

1961

RUANDA-URUNDI

[Burundi, Rwanda]

E central Africa. Former Belgian colony. *Area:* 10,169 sq. mi. (the size of Maryland). *Pop.:* 4,955,000. *Cap.:* Kigali. *Langs.:* French, Kinyarwandu and Swahili. *Money:* 100 centimes = 1 franc.

1931

1966

1965

BOLIVIA

Central South America. *Area:* 424,162 sq. mi. (the size of Texas and California combined). *Pop.:* 5,213,000. *Caps.:* Suere and La Paz. *Langs.:* | Spanish, Quechua and Aymara. *Money:* 100 centavos = 1 peso.

1931

1933

1939

1943

1946

1953

1962

1962

BRAZIL

[Brasil]

South America. *Area:* 3,286,470 sq. mi. (a little larger than the United States excluding Alaska and Hawaii). *Pop.:* 119,175,000. *Cap.:* Brasilia.

Off. Lang.: Portuguese. *Money:* 1000 reis = 1 milreis; 100 centavos = 1 cruzeiro.

1922–23

1929

1931–34

1941–42

1941–42

1954–56

1958

1958

1960

1963

1972–74

BURMA

SE Asia. Formerly part of British India. *Area:* 261,789 sq. mi. (nearly as large as Texas). *Pop.:* 33,590,000. *Cap.:* Rangoon. *Langs.:* Burmese and

English. *Money:* 12 pies = 1 anna; 15 annas = 1 rupee; since 1953, 100 pyas = 1 kyat.

1937

1938

1949

1964

CAMBODIA

[Cambodge,
République Khmère,
Democratic Kampuchea]

SE Asia. Former protectorate of France. *Area:* 69,900 sq. mi. (the size of Missouri). *Pop.:* 5,767,000. *Cap.:* Phnom Penh. *Langs.:* Khmer

and French. *Money:* 100 cents = 1 piaster; since 1955, 100 sen = 1 riel.

1959

1972

1972

19

BULGARIA

SW Europe. *Area:* 42,829 sq. mi. (slightly larger than Tennessee). *Pop.:* 8,827,000. *Cap.:* Sofia.

Langs.: Bulgarian, Turkish and Greek. *Money:* 100 stotinki = 1 lev.

1889

1896

1901–06

1911

1918–19

1930

1939

1946

1968

1968

20

CHILE

SW South America. *Area:* 286,396 sq. mi. (larger than Texas). *Pop.:* 10,848,000. *Cap.:* Santiago.

Lang.: Spanish. *Money:* 100 centesimos = 1 escudo.

1905–09

1929

1938–40

1956

1966

21

ESTONIA
[Eesti]

Socialist republic of the Soviet Union, N Europe. As an independent republic, it issued its own stamps from 1918 to 1940.

1922–24

1928–29

1936–39

| COLOMBIA | South America. *Area:* 455,355 sq. mi. (larger than Texas and California combined). *Pop.:* | 26,205,000. *Cap.:* Bogota. *Lang.:* Spanish. *Money:* 100 centavos = 1 peso. |

1932

1936

1939

1945

1947

1956

1957

1968

| COSTA RICA | Central America. *Area:* 19,653 sq. mi. (slightly smaller than West Virginia). *Pop.:* 2,184,000. | *Cap.:* San Jose. *Lang.:* Spanish. *Money:* 100 centimos = 1 colon. |

1937

1947

1952

1956

1959

| CUBA | West Indies. *Area:* 44,218 sq. mi. (nearly as large as Pennsylvania). *Pop.:* 9,824,000. *Cap.:* Havana. *Lang.:* Spanish. *Money:* 100 centavos = 1 peso. |

1917–31

1936

1956

CHINA

[People's Republic of China (mainland China)]

Central and E Asia. *Area:* 3,691,502 sq. mi. (slightly larger than the United States). *Pop.:* 1,012,197,000. *Cap.:* Peking. *Off. Lang.:* Chinese. *Money:* 100 fen = 1 yuan.

1923

1931–37

1940

1941

1942–43

1946–47

1946

1947

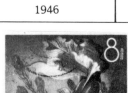
1960

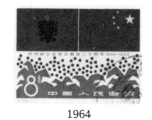
1964

CHINA

[Republic of China (Taiwan)]

Island of Formosa in South China Sea. Split from the mainland government in 1949. *Area:* 13,592 sq. mi. (the size of Maryland and Delaware combined). *Pop.:* 17,456,000. *Cap.:* Taipei. *Off. Lang.:* Chinese. *Money:* 100 cents = 1 yuan.

1953

1954

1956

1961

1972

1974

CZECHOSLOVAKIA

[Ceskoslovensko]

Central Europe. *Area:* 49,371 sq. mi. (the size of New York). *Pop.:* 15,239,000. *Cap.:* | Prague. *Langs.:* Czech, Slovak and Hungarian. *Money.:* 100 halers = 1 koruna.

1918–19		1919–20	1920
1920	1920–25		1925
1930	1930	1936–37	
	1945	1945–46	1949
1952	1953		1957
1958	1968		

28 BOHEMIA and MORAVIA [Cechy a Moravia]   A German Protectorate from 1939 to 1945.

	1942	1939–40	1943

29 SLOVAKIA   [Slovensko]   A nominally independent republic from 1939 to 1945.

1940–43	1943	1944	

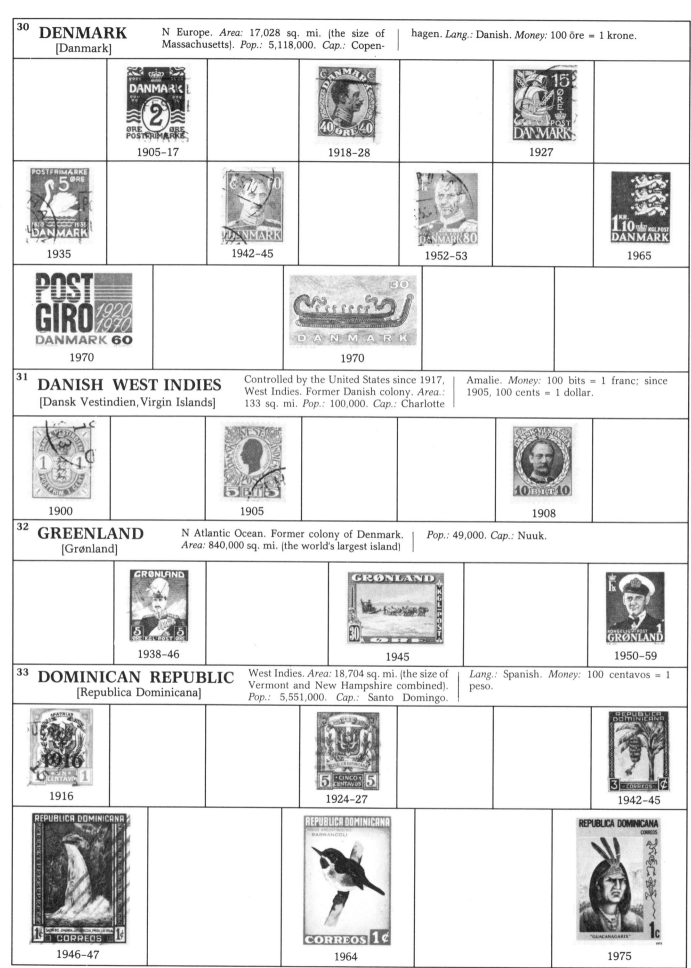

30 DENMARK
[Danmark]

N Europe. *Area:* 17,028 sq. mi. (the size of Massachusetts). *Pop.:* 5,118,000. *Cap.:* Copen-

hagen. *Lang.:* Danish. *Money:* 100 öre = 1 krone.

1905–17

1918–28

1927

1935

1942–45

1952–53

1965

1970

1970

31 DANISH WEST INDIES
[Dansk Vestindien, Virgin Islands]

Controlled by the United States since 1917, West Indies. Former Danish colony. *Area:* 133 sq. mi. *Pop.:* 100,000. *Cap.:* Charlotte

Amalie. *Money:* 100 bits = 1 franc; since 1905, 100 cents = 1 dollar.

1900

1905

1908

32 GREENLAND
[Grønland]

N Atlantic Ocean. Former colony of Denmark. *Area:* 840,000 sq. mi. (the world's largest island)

Pop.: 49,000. *Cap.:* Nuuk.

1938–46

1945

1950–59

33 DOMINICAN REPUBLIC
[Republica Dominicana]

West Indies. *Area:* 18,704 sq. mi. (the size of Vermont and New Hampshire combined). *Pop.:* 5,551,000. *Cap.:* Santo Domingo.

Lang.: Spanish. *Money:* 100 centavos = 1 peso.

1916

1924–27

1942–45

1946–47

1964

1975

20

34

ECUADOR

NW South America. *Area:* 105,685 sq. mi. (the size of Colorado). *Pop.:* 7,763,000. *Cap.:* Quito. *Lang.:* Spanish. *Money:* 100 centavos = 1 sucre.

1911–13

1920

1935

1943–45

1948

1956

1964

1965

35

EGYPT

[Égypte, United Arab Republic]

N Africa. *Area:* 363,250 sq. mi. (the size of Texas and New Mexico combined). *Pop.:* 40,993,000. *Cap.:* Cairo. *Lang.:* Arabic. *Money:* 40 paras = 1 piastre; since 1888, 1000 milliemes = 100 piastres = 1 pound.

1914

1921–22

1923–24

1937–44

1939–46

1944–46

1957

1946

1965

1965

36			
ETHIOPIA [Abyssinia, Éthiopie]	NE Africa. Formerly an empire. *Area:* 457,142 sq. mi. (about four-fifths the size of Alaska). *Pop.:* 31,780,000. *Cap.:* Addis Ababa. *Off. Lang.:* Am-	haric. *Money:* 40 paras = 1 piastre; since 1936, 100 centimes = 1 taler.	

Ethiopia stamps:

1928

1931

1942–44

1949–51

1969

37			
FINLAND [Suomi]	N Europe. *Area:* 130,119 sq. mi. (slightly smaller than Montana). *Pop.:* 4,764,000. *Cap.:* Helsinki.	*Off. Langs.:* Finnish and Swedish. *Money:* 100 pennis = 1 markka.	

1917–29

1925–29

1930

1937

1942

1957–58

1969

38			
HAITI	West Indies. *Area:* 10,714 sq. mi. (the size of Maryland). *Pop.:* 5,670,000. *Cap.:* Port-au-Prince.	*Langs.:* French and Créole. *Money:* 100 centimes = 1 gourde.	

1933

1963

1974

FRANCE

W Europe. *Area:* 212,973 sq. mi. (four-fifths the size of Texas). *Pop.:* 53,470,000. *Cap.:* Paris. *Lang.:* French. *Money:* 100 centimes = 1 franc.

1906–07	1923–26	1924–27
1930	1932	1936
1937	1938–39	1938–39
1941	1943	1947
1951	1953	
1957	1958	1961
1969	1970	

40

FRENCH GUIANA
[Guyane, Inini]

Overseas département of France, NE South America.

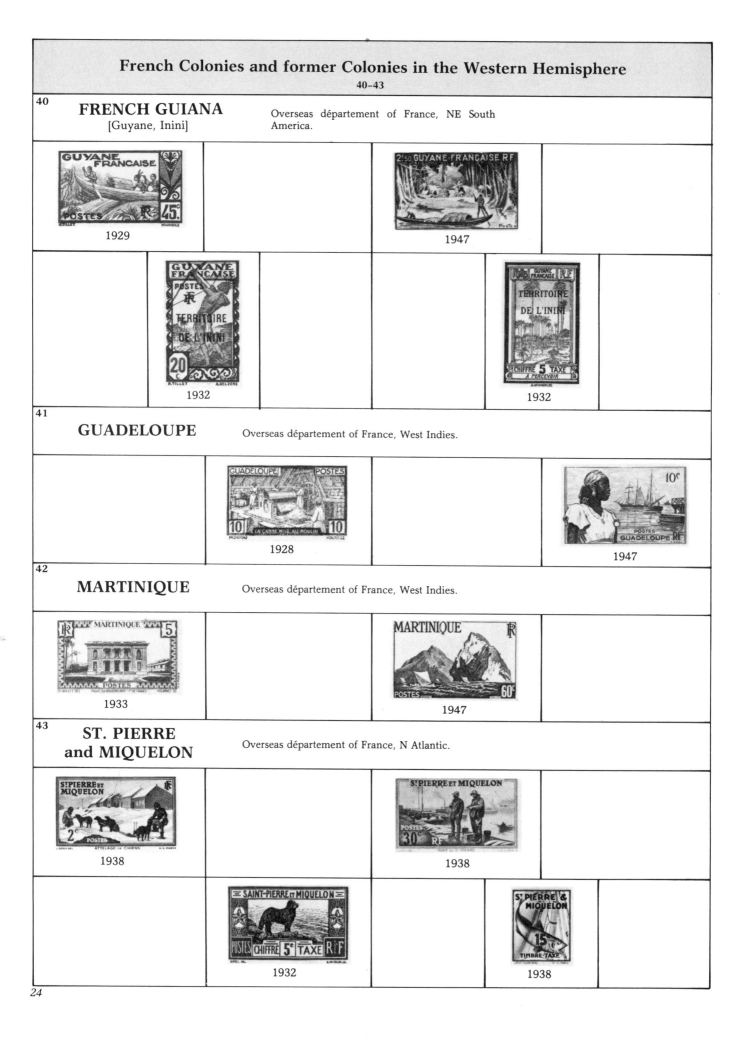

1929

1947

1932

1932

41

GUADELOUPE

Overseas département of France, West Indies.

1928

1947

42

MARTINIQUE

Overseas département of France, West Indies.

1933

1947

43

ST. PIERRE and MIQUELON

Overseas département of France, N Atlantic.

1938

1938

1932

1938

44

CAMEROON
[Cameroun]

Former French mandate, central Africa.

1946

1962

45

CENTRAL AFRICAN REPUBLIC and UBANGI

[Ubangi-Shari, République Centrafricaine]   Former French colony, central Africa.

1924

1963

46

CHAD
[Tchad]

Former French colony, central Africa.

1930

1967

47

DAHOMEY
[Benin]

Formerly part of French West Africa, W Africa.

1940

1968

48

CONGO

[République du Congo, Moyen-Congo]   Former French colony, central Africa.

1933

1961

49

FRENCH EQUATORIAL AFRICA

[Afrique Équatoriale Française]   Former French colony, W Africa.

1937

1946

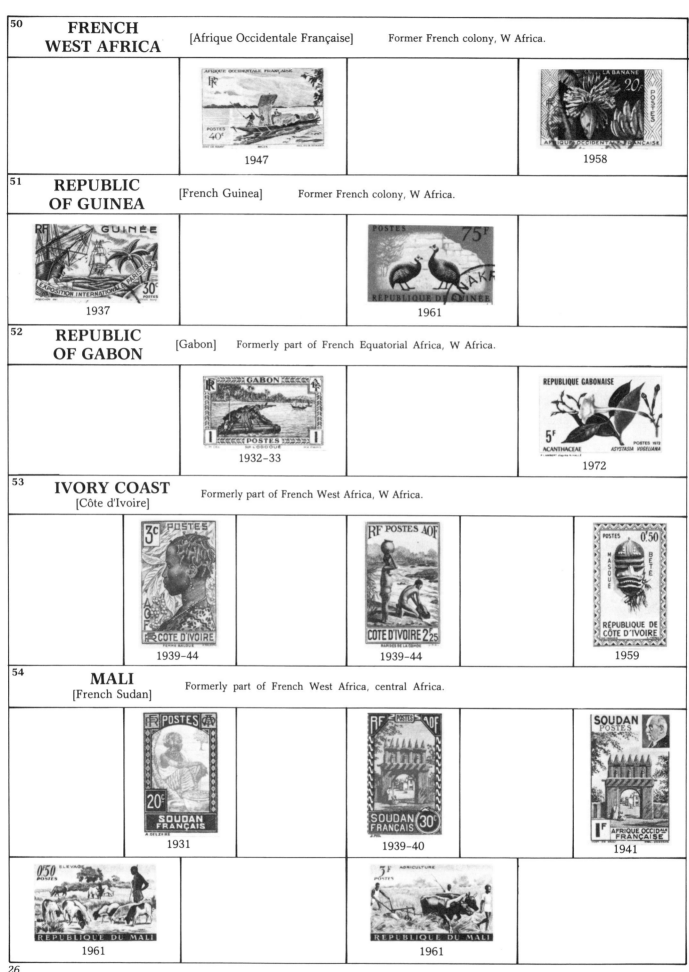

50 FRENCH WEST AFRICA [Afrique Occidentale Française] Former French colony, W Africa.

1947

1958

51 REPUBLIC OF GUINEA [French Guinea] Former French colony, W Africa.

1937

1961

52 REPUBLIC OF GABON [Gabon] Formerly part of French Equatorial Africa, W Africa.

1932–33

1972

53 IVORY COAST [Côte d'Ivoire] Formerly part of French West Africa, W Africa.

1939–44

1939–44

1959

54 MALI [French Sudan] Formerly part of French West Africa, central Africa.

1931

1939–40

1941

1961

1961

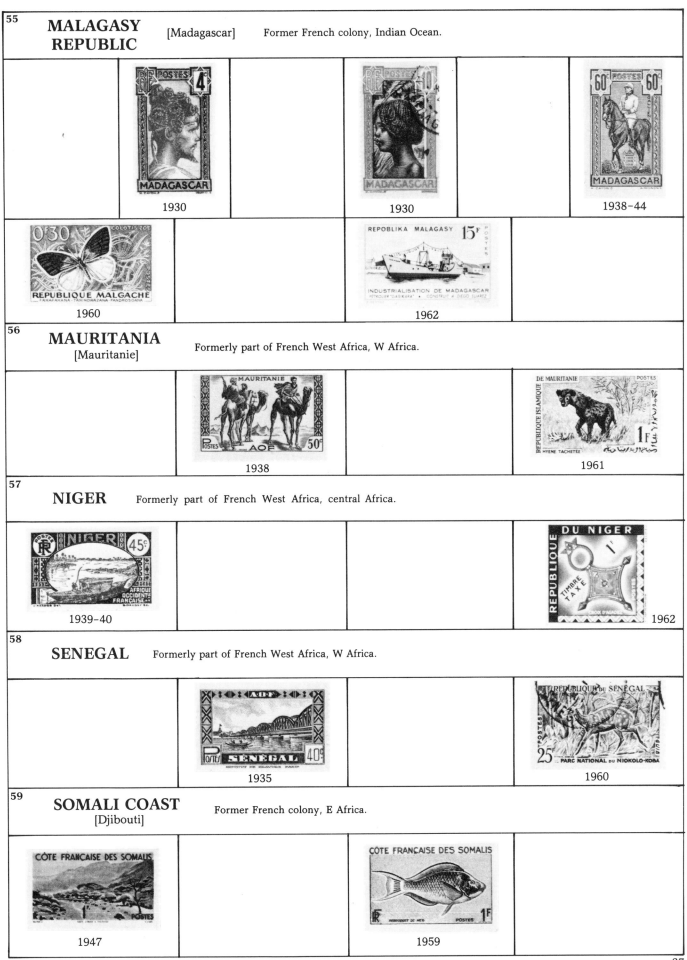

55

MALAGASY REPUBLIC

[Madagascar]   Former French colony, Indian Ocean.

1930	1930	1938–44
1960	1962	

56

MAURITANIA
[Mauritanie]   Formerly part of French West Africa, W Africa.

1938	1961	

57

NIGER   Formerly part of French West Africa, central Africa.

1939–40		1962

58

SENEGAL   Formerly part of French West Africa, W Africa.

1935	1960	

59

SOMALI COAST
[Djibouti]   Former French colony, E Africa.

1947	1959

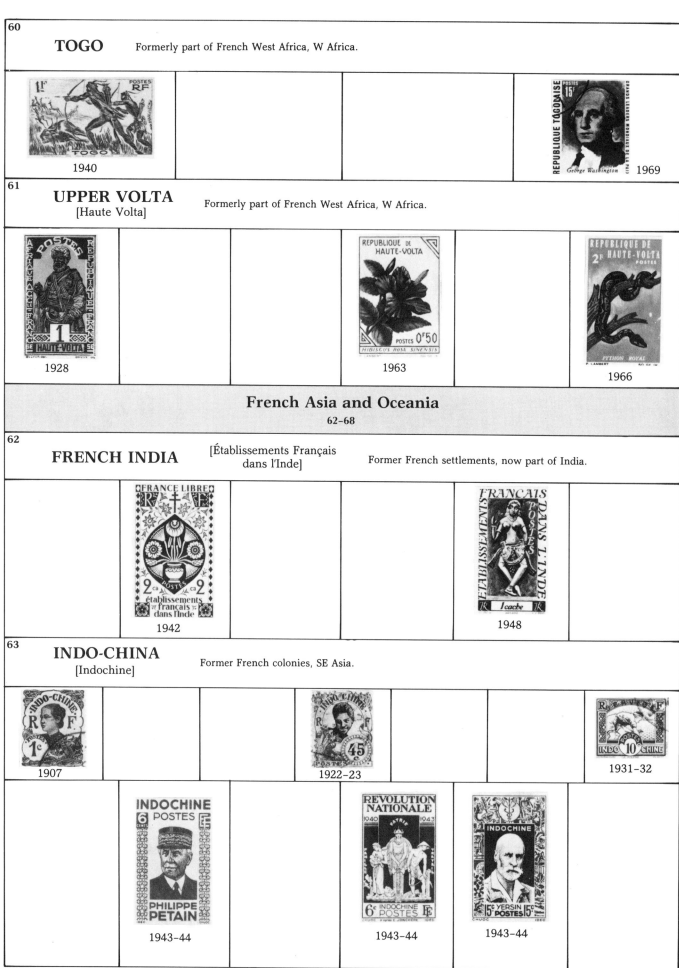

60

TOGO Formerly part of French West Africa, W Africa.

1940

1969

61

UPPER VOLTA
[Haute Volta] Formerly part of French West Africa, W Africa.

1928

1963

1966

French Asia and Oceania
62–68

62

FRENCH INDIA [Établissements Français dans l'Inde] Former French settlements, now part of India.

1942

1948

63

INDO-CHINA
[Indochine] Former French colonies, SE Asia.

1907

1922–23

1931–32

1943–44

1943–44

1943–44

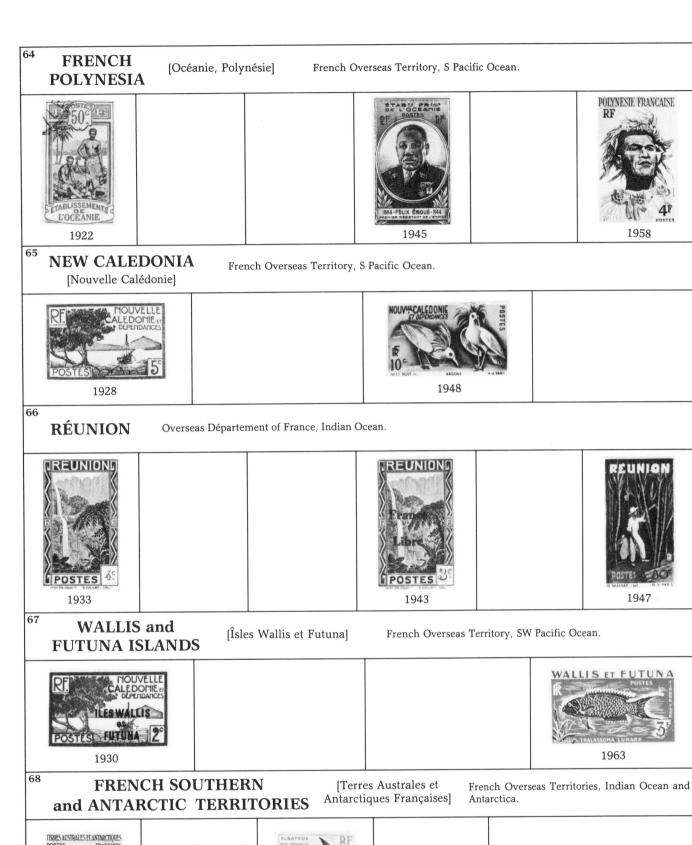

64 FRENCH
POLYNESIA   [Océanie, Polynésie]   French Overseas Territory, S Pacific Ocean.

1922   1945   1958

65 NEW CALEDONIA   French Overseas Territory, S Pacific Ocean.
[Nouvelle Calédonie]

1928   1948

66 RÉUNION   Overseas Département of France, Indian Ocean.

1933   1943   1947

67 WALLIS and
FUTUNA ISLANDS   [Îsles Wallis et Futuna]   French Overseas Territory, SW Pacific Ocean.

1930   1963

68 FRENCH SOUTHERN
and ANTARCTIC TERRITORIES   [Terres Australes et
Antarctiques Françaises]   French Overseas Territories, Indian Ocean and
Antarctica.

1956   1959
1959

GERMANY
[Deutsches Reich]

At the end of World War II in 1945, the Allies divided Germany into four zones. The three Western Zones were merged into the Federal Republic (West) and the Soviet Zone became the Democratic Republic (East).

1889–1900

1900

1916–19

1921–22

1921–23

1923

1923

1923

1923

1926

1928

1933–36

1936

1937

1938

1941–43

1946

FEDERAL REPUBLIC OF GERMANY
[West Germany, Bundesrepublik Deutschland]

Central Europe. *Area:* 95,815 sq. mi. (the size of Oregon). *Pop.:* 61,302,000. *Cap.:* Bonn. *Lang.:* German. *Money:* 100 Pfennigs = 1 Deutsche Mark.

1951–52

1954

1959

1959

1961–64

1964–65

1970–73

1970–73

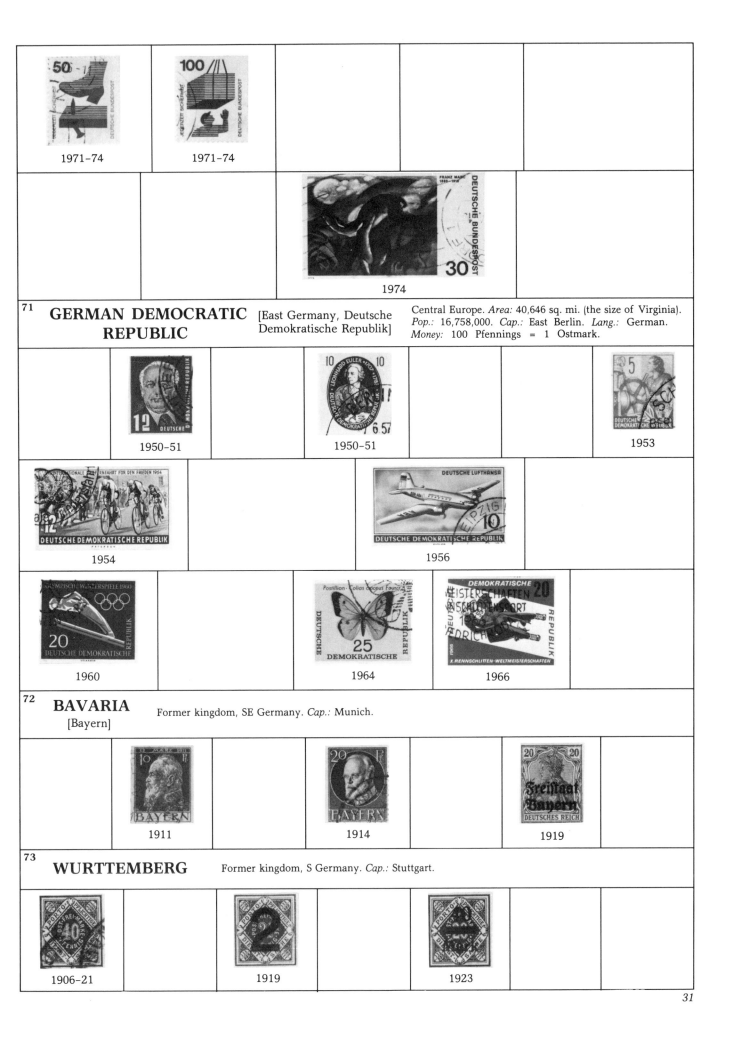 1971–74	100 1971–74			
		30 1974		

GERMAN DEMOCRATIC REPUBLIC

[East Germany, Deutsche Demokratische Republik]

Central Europe. *Area:* 40,646 sq. mi. (the size of Virginia). *Pop.:* 16,758,000. *Cap.:* East Berlin. *Lang.:* German. *Money:* 100 Pfennings = 1 Ostmark.

12 1950–51	10 1950–51		5 1953
1954		10 1956	
20 1960	25 1964	20 1966	

BAVARIA
[Bayern]

Former kingdom, SE Germany. *Cap.:* Munich.

1911	1914	1919

WURTTEMBERG

Former kingdom, S Germany. *Cap.:* Stuttgart.

40 1906–21	2 1919	1923

GREAT BRITAIN

NW of the European Continent in the N Atlantic. *Area:* 94,214 sq. mi. (slightly smaller than Oregon). *Pop.:* 55,901,000. *Cap.:* London. *Lang.:* English. *Money:* 12 pence = 1 shilling; 20 shillings = 1 pound; since 1970, 100 pence = 1 pound.

1887–92

1900

1902

1912–13

1922

1929

1934–36

1935

1936

1937–39

1940

1946–47

1953

1952–55

1957

1960

1965

1969

1971

75

CANADA

Self-governing dominion in the British Commonwealth of Nations, North America. *Area:* 3,831,033 sq. mi. (larger than the United States).

Pop.: 23,809,000. *Cap.:* Ottawa. *Off. Langs.:* English and French. *Money:* 100 cents = 1 dollar.

1902	1911–31	1927	1928–29
1932–33	1937–38	1937–38	1942–48
1942–48	1949–51	1953	
1954	1957		1962–64
1961–65	1967	1968	1973
1977	1978		

76

NEWFOUNDLAND

Former British Dominion, became the tenth province of the Dominion of Canada in 1949.

1911	1928	1937	

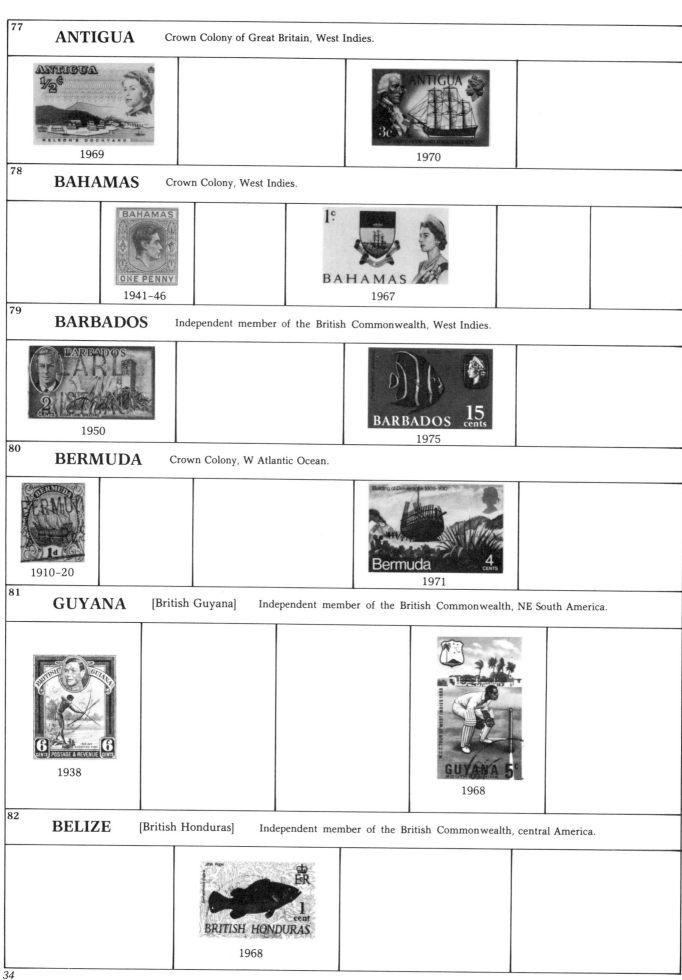

77

ANTIGUA

Crown Colony of Great Britain, West Indies.

1969

1970

78

BAHAMAS

Crown Colony, West Indies.

1941–46

1967

79

BARBADOS

Independent member of the British Commonwealth, West Indies.

1950

1975

80

BERMUDA

Crown Colony, W Atlantic Ocean.

1910–20

1971

81

GUYANA

[British Guyana]   Independent member of the British Commonwealth, NE South America.

1938

1968

82

BELIZE

[British Honduras]   Independent member of the British Commonwealth, central America.

1968

83

CAYMAN ISLANDS   Crown Colony, West Indies.

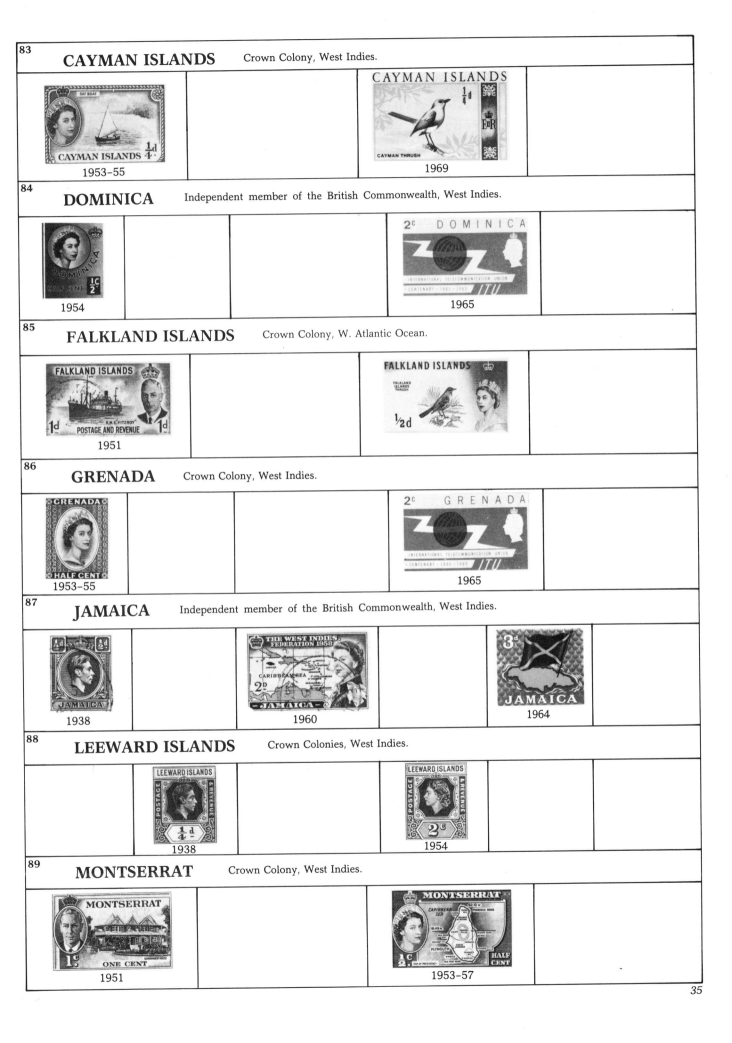

1953–55

1969

84

DOMINICA   Independent member of the British Commonwealth, West Indies.

1954

1965

85

FALKLAND ISLANDS   Crown Colony, W. Atlantic Ocean.

1951

86

GRENADA   Crown Colony, West Indies.

1953–55

1965

87

JAMAICA   Independent member of the British Commonwealth, West Indies.

1938

1960

1964

88

LEEWARD ISLANDS   Crown Colonies, West Indies.

1938

1954

89

MONTSERRAT   Crown Colony, West Indies.

1951

1953–57

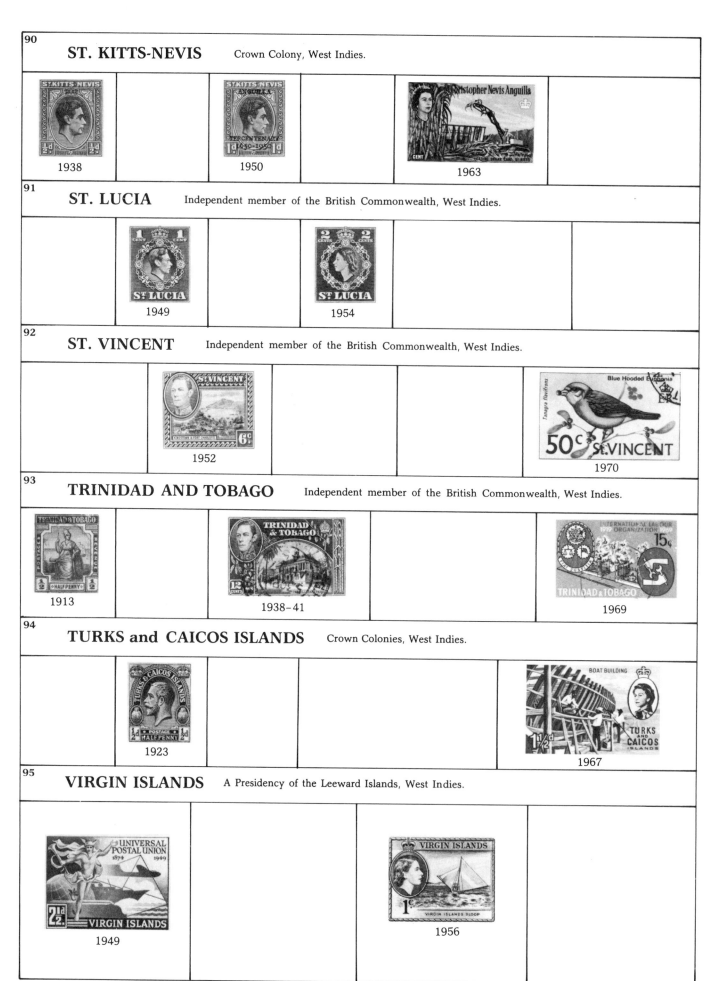

90

ST. KITTS-NEVIS   Crown Colony, West Indies.

1938

1950

1963

91

ST. LUCIA   Independent member of the British Commonwealth, West Indies.

1949

1954

92

ST. VINCENT   Independent member of the British Commonwealth, West Indies.

1952

1970

93

TRINIDAD AND TOBAGO   Independent member of the British Commonwealth, West Indies.

1913

1938–41

1969

94

TURKS and CAICOS ISLANDS   Crown Colonies, West Indies.

1923

1967

95

VIRGIN ISLANDS   A Presidency of the Leeward Islands, West Indies.

1949

1956

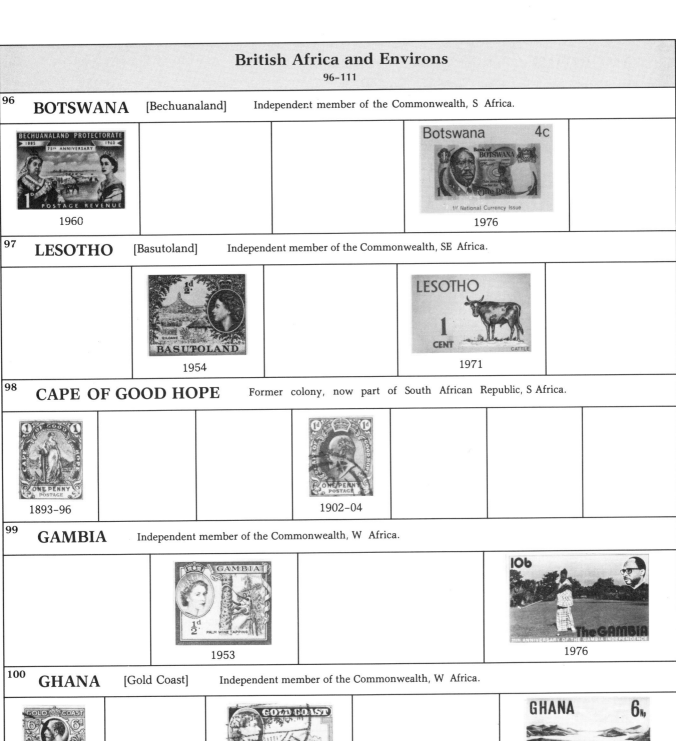

96 BOTSWANA [Bechuanaland] Independent member of the Commonwealth, S Africa.

1960   1976

97 LESOTHO [Basutoland] Independent member of the Commonwealth, SE Africa.

1954   1971

98 CAPE OF GOOD HOPE Former colony, now part of South African Republic, S Africa.

1893–96   1902–04

99 GAMBIA Independent member of the Commonwealth, W Africa.

1953   1976

100 GHANA [Gold Coast] Independent member of the Commonwealth, W Africa.

1928   1952–54   1976

101 KENYA, UGANDA and TANZANIA [Tanganyika] Independent members of the Commonwealth, E Africa.

1935   1953–59   1960–61   1963

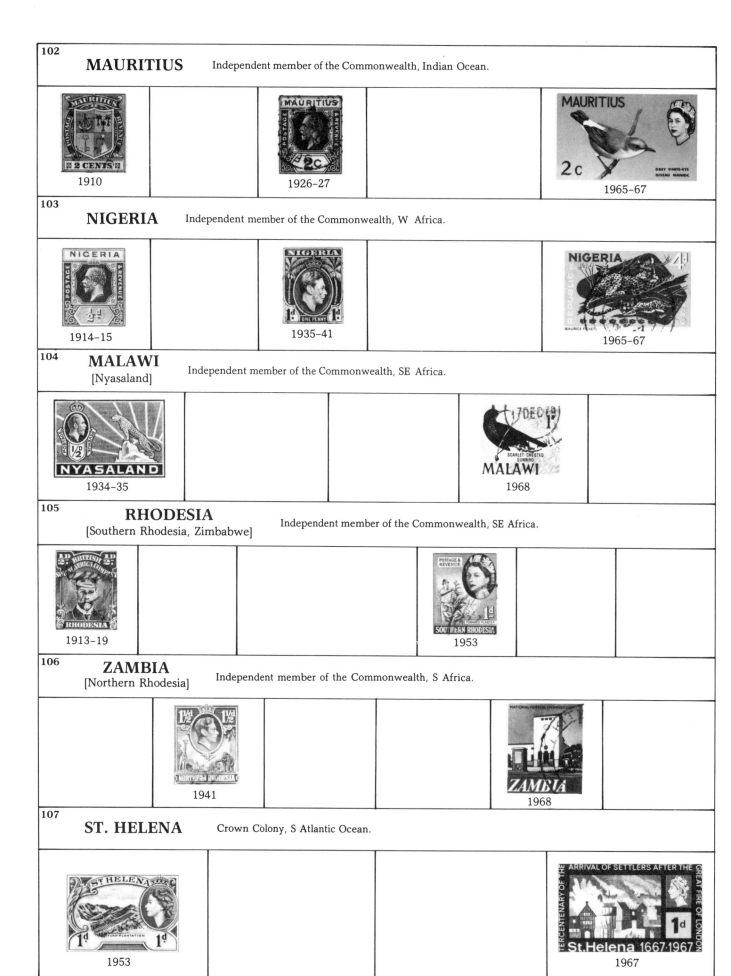

102

MAURITIUS   Independent member of the Commonwealth, Indian Ocean.

1910   1926–27   1965–67

103

NIGERIA   Independent member of the Commonwealth, W Africa.

1914–15   1935–41   1965–67

104

MALAWI
[Nyasaland]   Independent member of the Commonwealth, SE Africa.

1934–35   1968

105

RHODESIA
[Southern Rhodesia, Zimbabwe]   Independent member of the Commonwealth, SE Africa.

1913–19   1953

106

ZAMBIA
[Northern Rhodesia]   Independent member of the Commonwealth, S Africa.

1941   1968

107

ST. HELENA   Crown Colony, S Atlantic Ocean.

1953   1967

108

SIERRA LEONE   Independent member of the Commonwealth, W Africa.

1938		1956	

109

SOUTH WEST AFRICA   [Namibia]   Disputed territory, SW Africa. Granted independence by the United Nations, claimed by South African Republic.

1931	1954		

110

REPUBLIC OF SOUTH AFRICA
[Union of South Africa]

S Africa. Former dominion in the British Commonwealth. *Area:* 471,819 sq. mi. (four-fifths the size of Alaska). *Pop.:* 27,799,000. *Caps.:* Pretoria, Bloemfontein, Cape Town. *Langs.:* Afrikaans, English and Bantu. *Money:* 20 shillings = 1 pound; since 1961, 100 cents = 1 rand.

	1913–22	1926–27 1926–27	
1936	1940	1945	
1949		1964	
	1966	1972–74	

111

UGANDA   Independent nation since 1964, E Africa.

1898		1967	

112

AUSTRALIA

Self-governing dominion in the British Commonwealth, E Indian Ocean, W Pacific Ocean. *Area:* 2,965,368 sq. mi. (almost as large as the United States excluding Alaska and Hawaii). *Pop.:* 14,417,000. *Cap.:* Canberra. *Lang.:* English. *Money:* 12 pence = 1 shilling; since 1966, 100 cents = 1 dollar.

1913

1914–23

1935

1937–38

1937–38

1942

1947–48

1956–57

1959–60

1965

1970

113

CYPRUS

Independent member of the Commonwealth, Mediterranean Sea.

1924

1937

1955

1962

1972

114

FIJI

Crown Colony, W South Pacific.

1954–56

1956

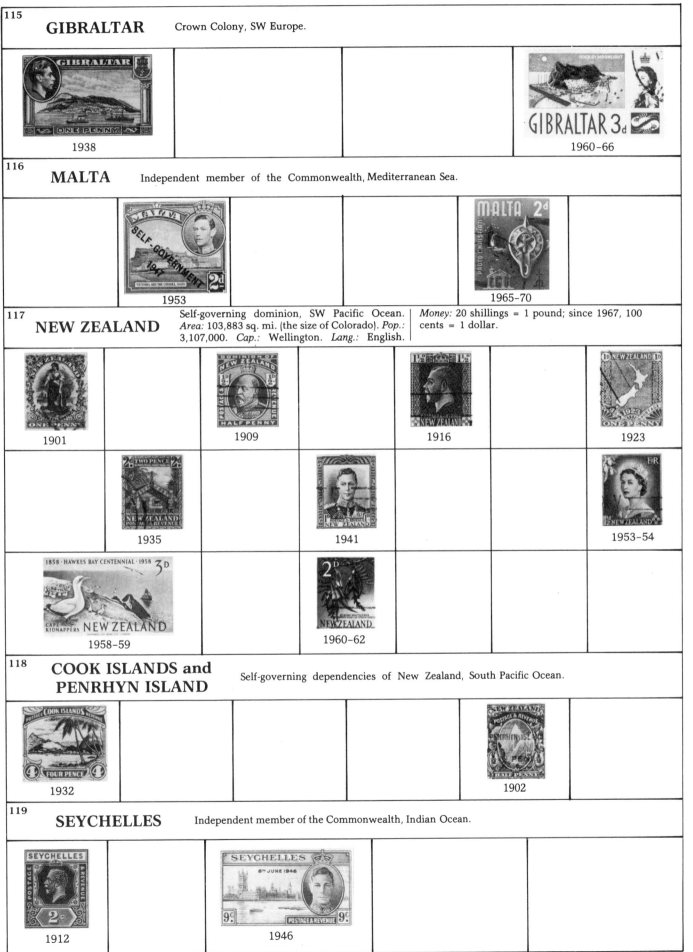

115

GIBRALTAR Crown Colony, SW Europe.

1938

GIBRALTAR 3d 1960–66

116

MALTA Independent member of the Commonwealth, Mediterranean Sea.

1953

1965–70

117

NEW ZEALAND Self-governing dominion, SW Pacific Ocean. *Area:* 103,883 sq. mi. (the size of Colorado). *Pop.:* 3,107,000. *Cap.:* Wellington. *Lang.:* English. | *Money:* 20 shillings = 1 pound; since 1967, 100 cents = 1 dollar.

1901

1909

1916

1923

1935

1941

1953–54

1958–59

1960–62

118

COOK ISLANDS and PENRHYN ISLAND Self-governing dependencies of New Zealand, South Pacific Ocean.

1932

1902

119

SEYCHELLES Independent member of the Commonwealth, Indian Ocean.

1912

1946

120

PAKISTAN

S central Asia. Formerly part of British India. *Area:* 342,750 sq. mi. (larger than Texas). *Pop.:* | 84,075,000. *Cap.:* Karachi. *Off. Langs.:* Urdu and English. *Money:* 100 paisas = 1 ruppee.

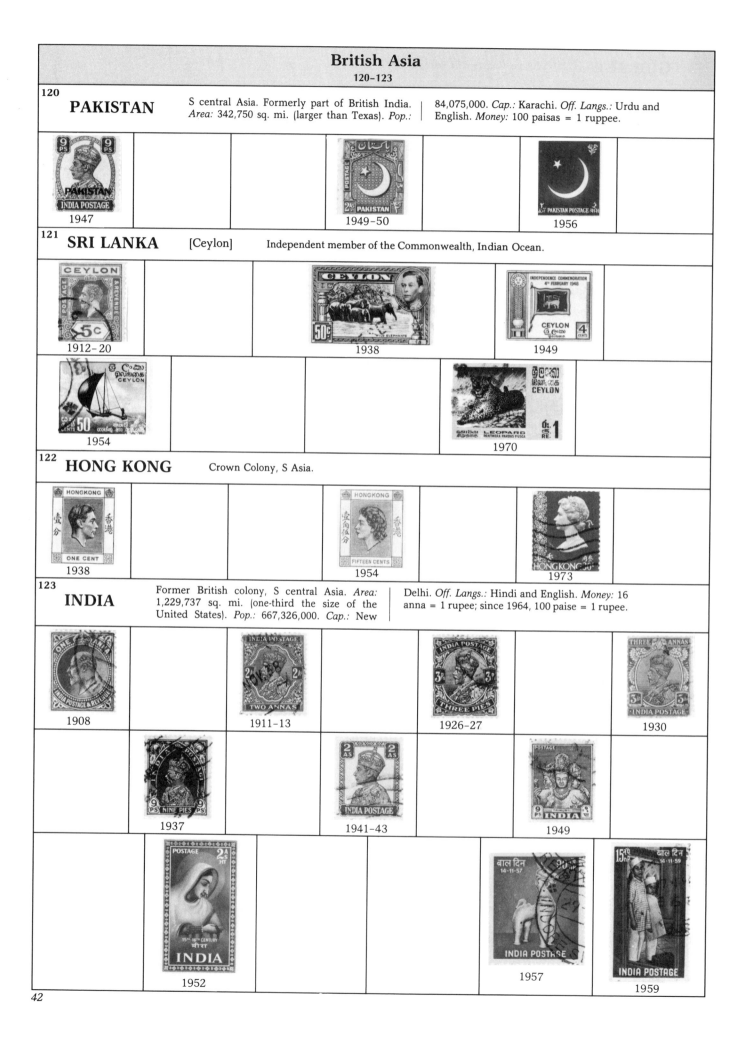

1947   1949–50   1956

121

SRI LANKA

[Ceylon]   Independent member of the Commonwealth, Indian Ocean.

1912–20   1938   1949

1954   1970

122

HONG KONG

Crown Colony, S Asia.

1938   1954   1973

123

INDIA

Former British colony, S central Asia. *Area:* 1,229,737 sq. mi. (one-third the size of the United States). *Pop.:* 667,326,000. *Cap.:* New | Delhi. *Off. Langs.:* Hindi and English. *Money:* 16 anna = 1 rupee; since 1964, 100 paise = 1 rupee.

1908   1911–13   1926–27   1930

1937   1941–43   1949

1952   1957   1959

 1965		 1975–79	

INDIAN STATES

Gwailor			Jhind

 1899	 1942–48	 1903–09	 1913–14

Patiala		Travancore	

 1932	 1938–42	 1939	

FEDERATION OF MALAYSIA, SINGAPORE, FEDERATED MALAY STATES, STRAITS SETTLEMENTS

Independent members of the Commonwealth, SE Asia.

 1922–32	 1904–08	 1950	

 1951	 1949	 1938–40	 1925

 1963	 1965	 1963–67	 1962–67

GREECE

S Balkan Peninsula, SE Europe. *Area:* 50,547 sq. mi. (the size of New York State). *Pop.:* 9,444,000. | *Cap.:* Athens. *Lang.:* Greek. *Money:* 100 lepta = 1 drachma.

1901

1911

1927

1930

1937

1946

1949

1952

1956

1959

1977

GUATEMALA

Central America. *Area:* 42,042 sq. mi. (the size of Tennessee). *Pop.:* 6,849,000. *Cap.:* Guatemala City. *Langs.:* Spanish and Maya-Quiche dialects. *Money:* 100 centavos = 1 quetzal.

1935

1946

1952

1954

1966–67

1967

128			
HONDURAS	Central America. *Area:* 43,277 sq. mi. (slightly larger than Tennessee). *Pop.:* 3,645,000. *Cap.:*	Tegucigalpa. *Langs.:* Spanish and English. *Money:* 100 centavos = 1 lempira.	

REPUBLICA DE HONDURAS — V CENTENARIO ISABEL LA CATÓLICA — DESCUBRIMIENTO DE AMÉRICA — UN CENTAVO DE LEMPIRA
1952

1865–1965 CENTENARIO DEL SELLO POSTAL — FERROCARRIL NACIONAL — AEREO — REPUBLICA DE HONDURAS
1966

129			
ICELAND [Island]	N Atlantic Ocean. *Area:* 39,702 sq. mi. (the size of Virginia). *Pop.:* 226,000. *Cap.:* Reykavik. *Lang.:* Icelandic. *Money:* 100 aurar = 1 krona.		

ÍSLAND 3 AUR
1939–45

Reykjavik 1786 – 18 ágúst – 1961 — ÍSLAND 4 50 kr
1961

ÍSLAND 15 KR — HEIMSMEISTARA-EINVIGI Í SKÁK REYKJAVÍK — 1972
1972

130			
IRAQ	W Asia. *Area:* 172,000 sq. mi. (slightly larger than California). *Pop.:* 12,906,000. *Cap.:*	Baghdad. *Langs.:* Arabic and Kurdish. *Money:* 1000 fils = 1 dinar.	

IRAQ 30 FILS
1934

4 FILS IRAQ POSTAGE
1941–42

2 FILS REPUBLIC OF IRAQ POSTAGE
1967

131			
IRELAND [Eire]	E Atlantic Ocean. *Area:* 26,600 sq. mi. (the size of West Virginia). *Pop.:* 3,365,000. *Cap.:* Dublin.	*Langs.:* English and Gaelic. *Money:* 12 pence = 1 shilling; since 1971, 100 pence = 1 pound.	

éire 2 DÁ PINṠIN
1922–23

éire 2 DÁ PIṄGIN 1731–1931 CUMANN RÍOGA BAILE ÁṪA ĊLIAṪ
1931

éire 1941 I ĊUIMNE AISÉIRĠE 1916 2 DÁ PINṠIN
1941

éire CONRADH NA GAEDILGE 1893 CUBLAS NA HÉIRE AN CÉAD UACTARÁN ½ 1P
1943

AN CHROIS DHEARG 1863–1963 ÉIRE 1'3
1963

éire MAHATMA GANDHI 1869 1948 1'0 dren
1969

132			
JORDAN [Transjordan, Hashemite Kingdom of Jordan]	W Asia. *Area:* 37,297 sq. mi. (slightly larger than Indiana). *Pop.:* 3,189,000. *Cap.:* Amman. *Lang.:*	Arabic. *Money:* 10 milliemes = 1 piastre; since 1951, 1000 fils = 1 Jordan dinar.	

10 TRANSJORDAN MIL
1930

AIRMAIL 5 FILS THE HASHEMITE KINGDOM OF JORDAN
1954

60 FILS AIRMAIL
1967

HUNGARY
[Magyarorzag]

SE Europe. Part of the Austro-Hungarian Empire until 1918. *Area:* 35,919 sq. mi. (slightly smaller than Indiana). *Pop.:* 10,710,000. *Cap.:* Budapest.

Lang.: Hungarian. *Money:* 100 fillar = 1 korona; after 1926, 100 fillar = 1 pengo; since 1946, 100 fillér = 1 forint.

1904–08	1916	1919	1926–27
	1932	1939	1943–45
1945–46		1946	1946–47
1959	1962		

ISRAEL

W Asia. *Area:* 8,219 sq. mi. (the size of Massachusetts). *Pop.:* 3,783,000. *Cap.:* Jerusalem. *Langs.:* Hebrew, Arabic and various European and West Asian Languages. *Money:* 1000 mils = 1 Israel pound; 1960, 100 agorot = 1 Israel pound.

1948	1951		1953–56
1955–56	1957		1959
1964	1965		1971

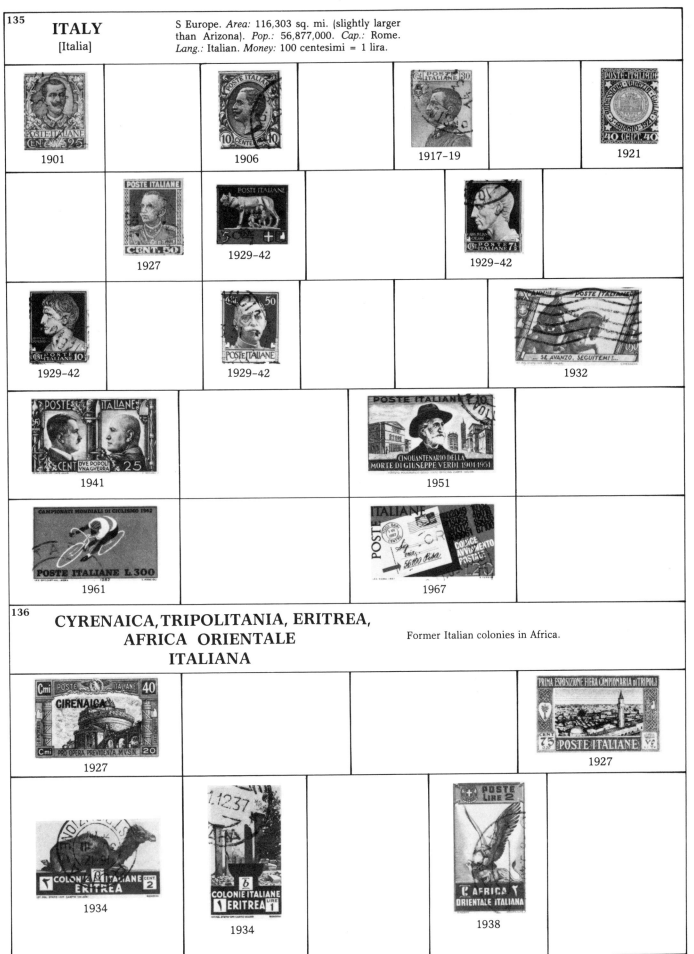

135 **ITALY**
[Italia]

S Europe. *Area:* 116,303 sq. mi. (slightly larger than Arizona). *Pop.:* 56,877,000. *Cap.:* Rome. *Lang.:* Italian. *Money:* 100 centesimi = 1 lira.

1901

1906

1917–19

1921

1927

1929–42

1929–42

1929–42

1929–42

1932

1941

1951

1961

1967

136 **CYRENAICA, TRIPOLITANIA, ERITREA, AFRICA ORIENTALE ITALIANA**

Former Italian colonies in Africa.

1927

1927

1934

1934

1938

IRAN
[Persia]

W Asia. *Area:* 636,363 sq. mi. (nearly two and one-half times the size of Texas). *Pop.:* 37,430,000. *Cap.:* Teheran. *Langs.:* Persian, | Turkish, Kurdish and Arabic. *Money:* 100 dinar = 1 rial; 20 rials = 1 pahlavi.

1894	1898	1904
1911	1915	1918
1926	1931–32	1933–39
1938–39	1944–46	
1962	1965	

JAPAN

NW Pacific Ocean. *Area:* 143,574 sq. mi. (slightly smaller than Montana). *Pop.:* 115,880,000. | *Cap.:* Tokyo. *Lang.:* Japanese. *Money:* 100 sen = 1 yen.

1899–1910	1913–25	1921–23	1924–37
	1934–36	1936–38	1937–40

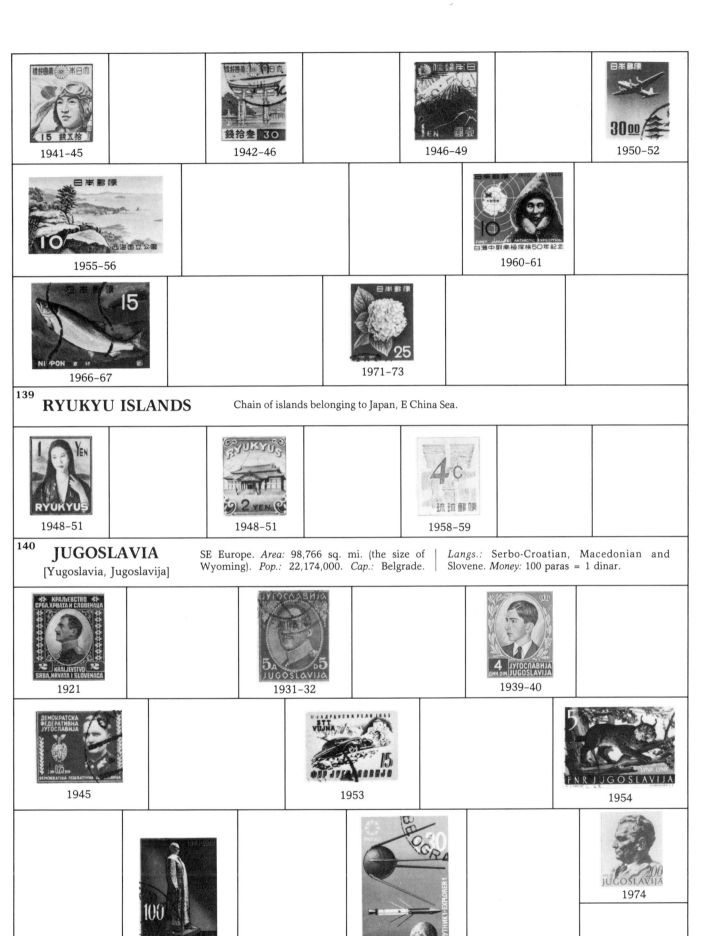

1941–45

1942–46

1946–49

1950–52

1955–56

1960–61

1966–67

1971–73

139 **RYUKYU ISLANDS** Chain of islands belonging to Japan, E China Sea.

1948–51

1948–51

1958–59

140 **JUGOSLAVIA**
[Yugoslavia, Jugoslavija]

SE Europe. *Area:* 98,766 sq. mi. (the size of Wyoming). *Pop.:* 22,174,000. *Cap.:* Belgrade. │ *Langs.:* Serbo-Croatian, Macedonian and Slovene. *Money:* 100 paras = 1 dinar.

1921

1931–32

1939–40

1945

1953

1954

1961

1967

1974

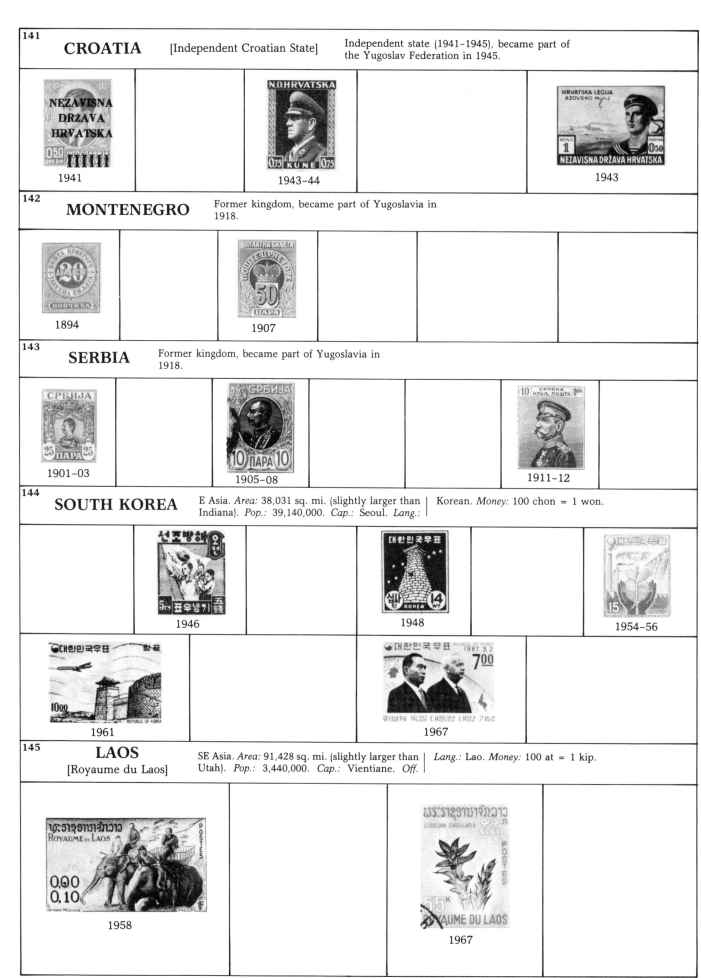

141

CROATIA   [Independent Croatian State]   Independent state (1941–1945), became part of the Yugoslav Federation in 1945.

1941

1943–44

1943

142

MONTENEGRO   Former kingdom, became part of Yugoslavia in 1918.

1894

1907

143

SERBIA   Former kingdom, became part of Yugoslavia in 1918.

1901–03

1905–08

1911–12

144

SOUTH KOREA   E Asia. *Area:* 38,031 sq. mi. (slightly larger than Indiana). *Pop.:* 39,140,000. *Cap.:* Seoul. *Lang.:* | Korean. *Money:* 100 chon = 1 won.

1946

1948

1954–56

1961

1967

145

LAOS   SE Asia. *Area:* 91,428 sq. mi. (slightly larger than Utah). *Pop.:* 3,440,000. *Cap.:* Vientiane. *Off.* | *Lang.:* Lao. *Money:* 100 at = 1 kip.
[Royaume du Laos]

1958

1967

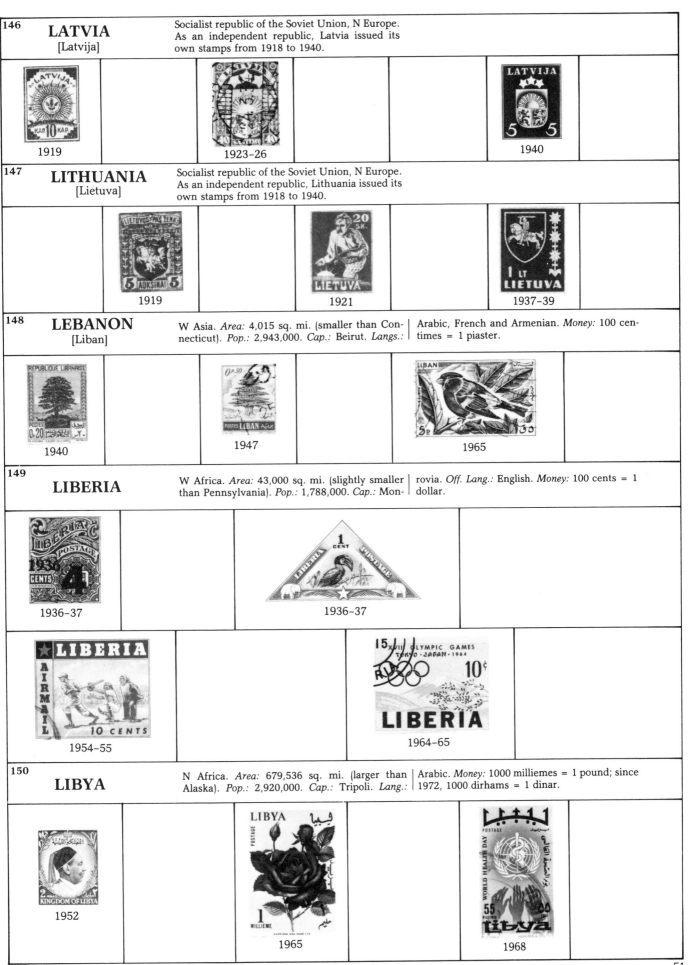

146 LATVIA
[Latvija]

Socialist republic of the Soviet Union, N Europe. As an independent republic, Latvia issued its own stamps from 1918 to 1940.

1919

1923–26

1940

147 LITHUANIA
[Lietuva]

Socialist republic of the Soviet Union, N Europe. As an independent republic, Lithuania issued its own stamps from 1918 to 1940.

1919

1921

1937–39

148 LEBANON
[Liban]

W Asia. *Area:* 4,015 sq. mi. (smaller than Connecticut). *Pop.:* 2,943,000. *Cap.:* Beirut. *Langs.:* Arabic, French and Armenian. *Money:* 100 centimes = 1 piaster.

1940

1947

1965

149 LIBERIA

W Africa. *Area:* 43,000 sq. mi. (slightly smaller than Pennsylvania). *Pop.:* 1,788,000. *Cap.:* Monrovia. *Off. Lang.:* English. *Money:* 100 cents = 1 dollar.

1936–37

1936–37

1954–55

1964–65

150 LIBYA

N Africa. *Area:* 679,536 sq. mi. (larger than Alaska). *Pop.:* 2,920,000. *Cap.:* Tripoli. *Lang.:* Arabic. *Money:* 1000 milliemes = 1 pound; since 1972, 1000 dirhams = 1 dinar.

1952

1965

1968

151						
## LIECHTENSTEIN		Central Europe. *Area:* 61 sq. mi. (the size of Washington, D.C.). *Pop.:* 26,000. *Cap.:* Vaduz. *Lang.:* German. *Money:* 100 rappen = 1 franc.				

1943

1954

1968

152			
## LUXEMBOURG	W Europe. *Area:* 999 sq. mi. (smaller than Rhode Island). *Pop.:* 358,000. *Cap.:* Luxembourg.	*Langs.:* French, German and Luxembourgish. *Money:* 100 centimes = 1 franc.

1944–46

1951–53

1960–64

153		
## MANCHURIA [Manchukuo]	Region of the People's Republic of China. Former independent state under Japanese influence (1932 to 1945), NE Asia.

1936–37

1937–42

1942–45

1942–45

154		
## MONACO	S Europe. *Area:* 600 acres. *Pop.:* 26,000. *Cap.:* Monaco. *Langs.:* French, Monégasque, Italian and English. *Money:* 100 centimes = 1 franc.

1926–33

1937–39

1941–46

1952

1956

1962

155		
## MONGOLIA	Central Asia. *Area:* 604,247 sq. mi. (more than twice the size of Texas). *Pop.:* 1,616,000. *Cap.:*	Ulan Bator. *Langs.:* Mongolian and Turkic. *Money:* 100 mungo = 1 Tughrik.

1932

1932

1958

MEXICO

Central America. *Area:* 761,601 sq. mi. (three times the size of Texas). *Pop.:* 65,770,000. *Cap.:* | Mexico City. *Off. Lang.:* Spanish. *Money:* 100 centimes = 1 peso.

1915	1917	1923
1934	1940	1945
1952	1954	1956–63
1962	1976	

MOROCCO
[Royaume du Maroc]

N Africa. *Area:* 171,953 sq. mi. (larger than California). *Pop.:* 20,368,000. *Cap.:* Rabat. *Langs.:* | Arabic, Berber and French. *Money:* 100 centimes = 1 franc.

1949	1955	1962

NETHERLANDS
[Nederland]

NW Europe. *Area:* 14,103 sq. mi. (the size of Massachusetts, Connecticut and Rhode Island combined). *Pop.:* 14,029,000. *Caps.:* Amsterdam | and The Hague. *Lang.:* Dutch. *Money:* 100 cents = 1 guilder or florin.

1899	1901–1910	1923	1924–26
	1926–27	1937	1940

1943–44

1947–48

1952

1962

1964

159 NEDERLANDS ANTILLES

[Curacao, Aruba, Bonaire]

Former Dutch colony, integral part of the Kingdom of the Netherlands, West Indies.

1936

1941–42

1965

160 SURINAME

[Dutch Guiana]

Former Dutch colony, integral part of the Kingdom of the Netherlands. NE South America.

1936

1948

1950

161 DUTCH EAST INDIES   [Indonesia]   Former Dutch colony, W Pacific Ocean.

1912–40

1933–34

1938

162 INDONESIA

[United States of Indonesia]

Formerly the Dutch East Indies. *Area:* 735,268 sq. mi. (larger than the state of Alaska). *Pop.:* 148,085,000. *Cap.:* Jakarta. *Langs.:* Bahasa Indonesian and Javanese. *Money:* 100 sen = 1 rupiah.

1953

1962

1969

163 **NICARAGUA**	Central America. *Area:* 57,143 sq. mi. (slightly larger than Wisconsin). *Pop.:* 2,365,000. *Cap.:*	Mangua. *Langs.:* Spanish and English. *Money:* 100 centavos = 1 cordoba.	

1914

1927

1938

1949

1967

164 **NORWAY** [Norge]	N Europe. *Area:* 125,181 sq. mi. (slightly larger than New Mexico). *Pop.:* 4,074,000. *Cap.:* Oslo.	*Langs.:* Norwegian and Lapp. *Money:* 100 ore = 1 krone.	

1926–34

1932

1940

1947

1957

1969

165 **PANAMA**	Central America. *Area:* 29,306 sq. mi. (slightly larger than West Virginia). *Pop.:* 1,876,000. *Cap.:*	Panama City. *Langs.:* Spanish and English. *Money:* 100 centesimos = 1 balboa.	

1924

1955

1962

166 **PARAGUAY**	Central South America. *Area:* 157,047 sq. mi. (the size of California). *Pop.:* 3,117,000. *Cap.:* Asuncion. *Langs.:* Spanish and Guarani. *Money:*	100 centavos = 1 peso; since 1944, 100 centimos = 1 guarani.	

1942

1960

1961

167 PERU

W South America. *Area:* 496,222 sq. mi. (five-sixths the size of Alaska). *Pop.:* 17,164,000. *Cap.:* Lima. *Langs.:* Spanish, Quechua and Aymara. *Money:* 100 centavos = 1 sol.

1917–18	1924	1931	1932–33
1938		1952–53	1967

168 PHILIPPINES

W Pacific Ocean. *Area:* 115,831 sq. mi. (slightly larger than Nevada). *Pop.:* 47,678,000. *Cap.:* Manila. *Langs.:* Spanish, English and Filipino. *Money:* 100 centavos = 1 peso.

1906	1938–40		1940
1947	1956	1969	

169 POLAND
[Polska]

E Europe. *Area:* 120,359 sq. mi. (about the size of New Mexico). *Pop.:* 35,227,000. *Cap.:* Warsaw. *Lang.:* Polish. *Money:* 100 groszy = 1 zloty.

1927–31	1932–34	1935–37
1938–39	1945–46	1948–49
1958–59	1962	1971

| 170 **PORTUGAL** | SW Europe. *Area:* 35,340 sq. mi. (slightly smaller than Indiana). *Pop.:* 9,843,000. *Cap.:* Lisbon. | *Lang.:* Portuguese. *Money:* 100 centavos = 1 escudo. |

1922–23		1924		1926		1928–29
	1931–38		1935–36			1941
1952–56		1963				

Portuguese Colonies and former Colonies
171–173

171 ANGOLA
Former colony of Portugal, SW Africa.

1921		1931		1951	

172 AZORES
Possession of Portugal, E Atlantic Ocean.

	1918		1930		1918

173 MOZAMBIQUE
[Companhia de Moçambique]

Former colony of Portugal, SE Africa.

1921		1951			1935

174 **ROMANIA**

SE Europe. *Area:* 91,699 sq. mi. (slightly smaller than Oregon). *Pop.:* 22,057,000. *Cap.:* Bucharest. | *Langs.:* Romanian and Hungarian. *Money:* 100 bani = 1 leu.

1928–29

1930–31

1940–42

1946

1950

1955–56

1957

1965

1965

175 **RUSSIA**
[Union of Soviet Socialist Republics]

E Europe and N Asia. *Area:* 8,647,250 sq. mi. (nearly two and one-half times the size of the United States). *Pop.:* 262,436,000. *Cap.:* Moscow. | *Langs.:* Russian and other Slavic languages; and Altiac, Uralian and Caucasian languages. *Money:* 100 kopecks = 1 ruble.

1902–06

1909–12

1917

1919

1922–23

1925–26

1929–31

1935

1941

1943–46

1947

1958

1973

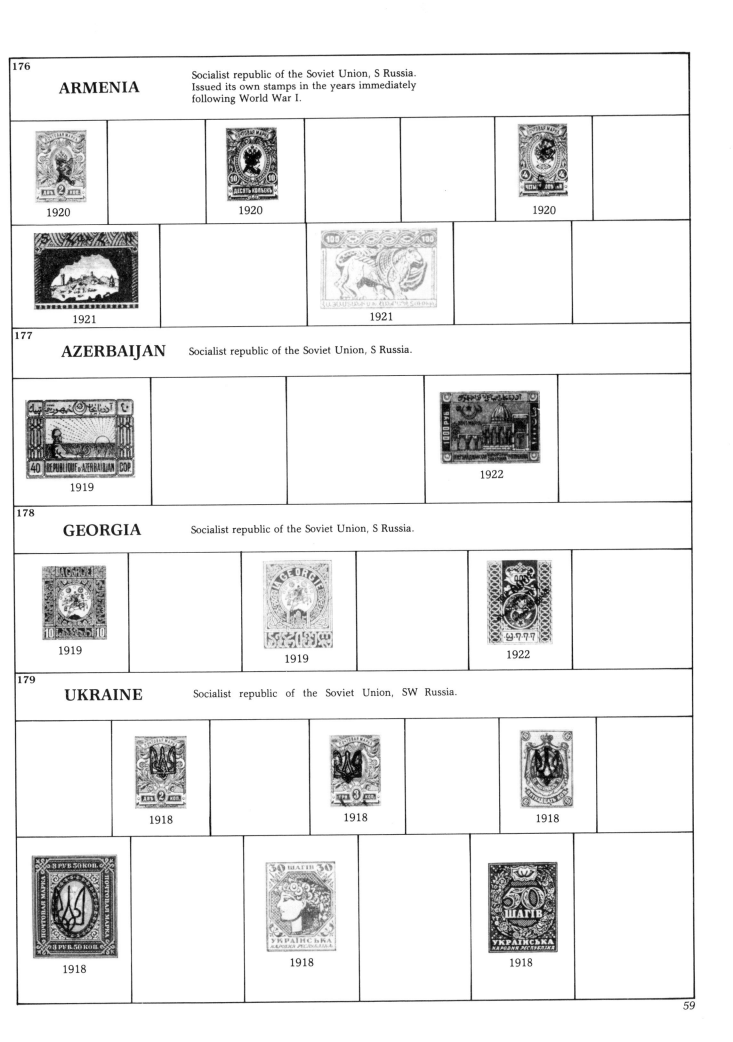

176

ARMENIA

Socialist republic of the Soviet Union, S Russia.
Issued its own stamps in the years immediately
following World War I.

1920

1920

1920

1921

1921

177

AZERBAIJAN

Socialist republic of the Soviet Union, S Russia.

1919

1922

178

GEORGIA

Socialist republic of the Soviet Union, S Russia.

1919

1919

1922

179

UKRAINE

Socialist republic of the Soviet Union, SW Russia.

1918

1918

1918

1918

1918

1918

180

EL SALVADOR

Central America. *Area:* 8,260 sq. mi. (the size of Massachusetts). *Pop.:* 4,622,000. *Cap.:* San | Salvador. *Lang.:* Spanish. *Money:* 100 centavos = 1 colon.

| 1912 | | 1934 | | 1963 |

181

SAN MARINO

N central Italy. *Area:* 38 sq. mi. *Pop.:* 21,000. *Cap.:* San Marino. *Lang.:* Italian. *Money:* 100 centesimi = 1 lira.

| 1949–50 | | | | 1962 |

182

SAUDI ARABIA

SW Asia. *Area:* 873,000 sq. mi. (one-fourth the size of the United States). *Pop.:* 9,292,000. *Cap.:* | Riyadh. *Lang.:* Arabic. *Money:* 20 piasters = 1 riyal.

| 1934–39 | | 1960–61 | | 1960–61 |

183

SPAIN
[España]

SW Europe. *Area:* 194,883 sq. mi. (the size of Colorado and Wyoming combined). *Pop.:* 37,077,000. *Cap.:* Madrid. *Langs.:* Spanish, | Basque and others. *Money:* 100 centimes = 1 peseta.

| 1922–26 | | 1930 | | 1931 |

| 1935 | | 1936–37 | | 1938–39 | | 1938–39 |

| 1948–50 | | 1954–56 | 1961 |

184

SPANISH MOROCCO   [Marruecos]   Former colony of Spain, N Africa.

| 1943 | | 1948 | |

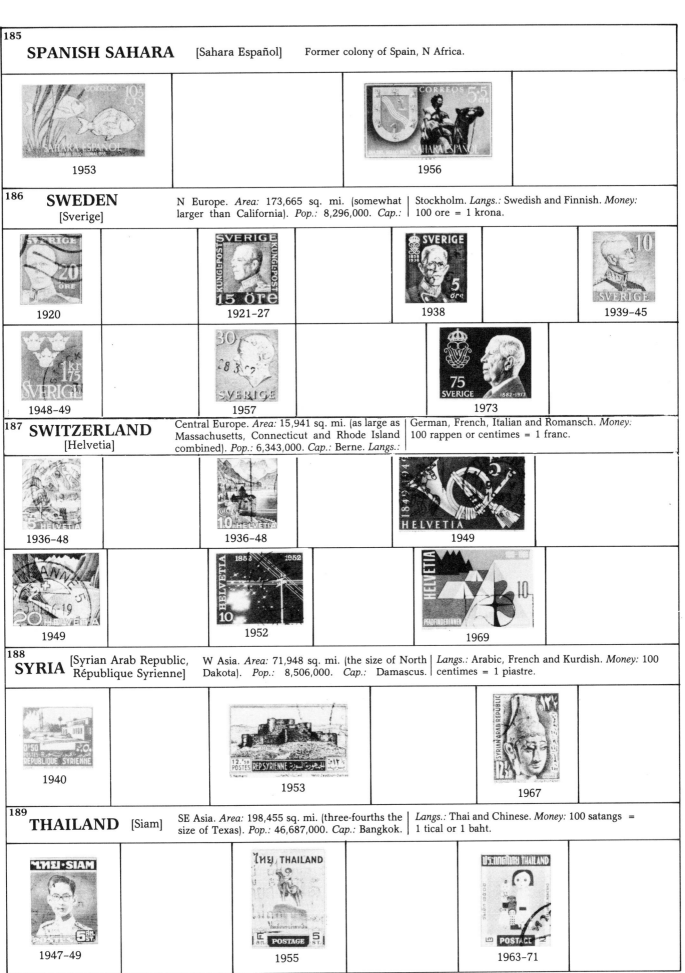

185

SPANISH SAHARA   [Sahara Español]   Former colony of Spain, N Africa.

1953		1956	

186

SWEDEN
[Sverige]

N Europe. *Area:* 173,665 sq. mi. (somewhat larger than California). *Pop.:* 8,296,000. *Cap.:* Stockholm. *Langs.:* Swedish and Finnish. *Money:* 100 ore = 1 krona.

1920	1921–27	1938	1939–45
1948–49	1957	1973	

187

SWITZERLAND
[Helvetia]

Central Europe. *Area:* 15,941 sq. mi. (as large as Massachusetts, Connecticut and Rhode Island combined). *Pop.:* 6,343,000. *Cap.:* Berne. *Langs.:* German, French, Italian and Romansch. *Money:* 100 rappen or centimes = 1 franc.

1936–48	1936–48	1949
1949	1952	1969

188

SYRIA [Syrian Arab Republic, République Syrienne]

W Asia. *Area:* 71,948 sq. mi. (the size of North Dakota). *Pop.:* 8,506,000. *Cap.:* Damascus. *Langs.:* Arabic, French and Kurdish. *Money:* 100 centimes = 1 piastre.

1940	1953	1967

189

THAILAND [Siam]

SE Asia. *Area:* 198,455 sq. mi. (three-fourths the size of Texas). *Pop.:* 46,687,000. *Cap.:* Bangkok. *Langs.:* Thai and Chinese. *Money:* 100 satangs = 1 tical or 1 baht.

1947–49	1955	1963–71

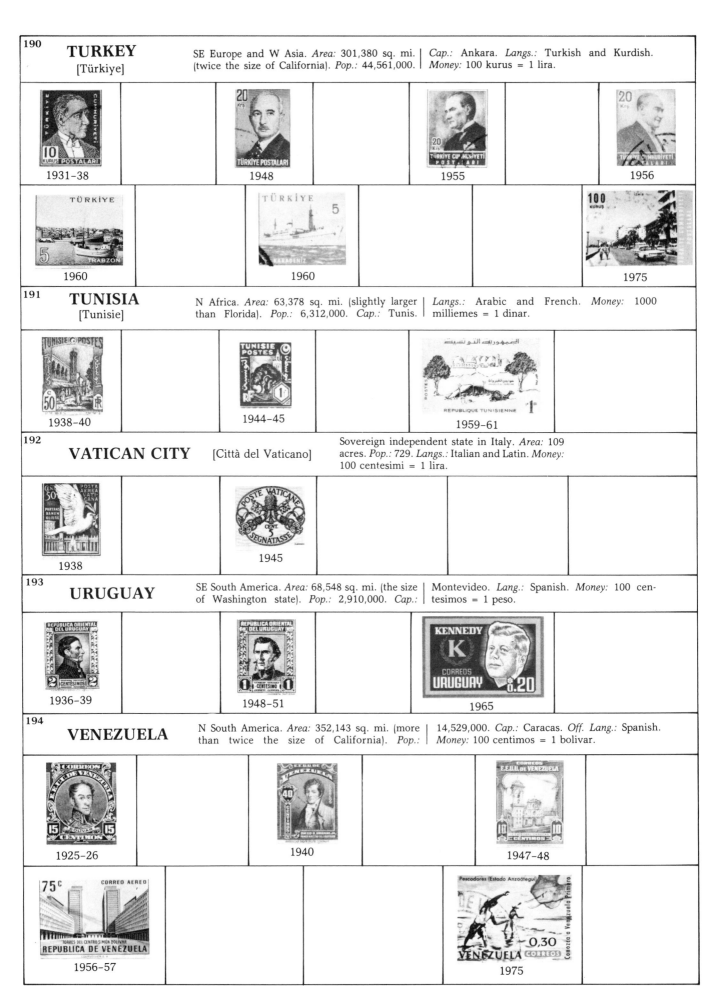

190   **TURKEY**
[Türkiye]

SE Europe and W Asia. *Area:* 301,380 sq. mi. (twice the size of California). *Pop.:* 44,561,000. | *Cap.:* Ankara. *Langs.:* Turkish and Kurdish. *Money:* 100 kurus = 1 lira.

1931–38   1948   1955   1956

1960   1960   1975

191   **TUNISIA**
[Tunisie]

N Africa. *Area:* 63,378 sq. mi. (slightly larger than Florida). *Pop.:* 6,312,000. *Cap.:* Tunis. | *Langs.:* Arabic and French. *Money:* 1000 milliemes = 1 dinar.

1938–40   1944–45   1959–61

192   **VATICAN CITY**   [Città del Vaticano]

Sovereign independent state in Italy. *Area:* 109 acres. *Pop.:* 729. *Langs.:* Italian and Latin. *Money:* 100 centesimi = 1 lira.

1938   1945

193   **URUGUAY**

SE South America. *Area:* 68,548 sq. mi. (the size of Washington state). *Pop.:* 2,910,000. *Cap.:* | Montevideo. *Lang.:* Spanish. *Money:* 100 centesimos = 1 peso.

1936–39   1948–51   1965

194   **VENEZUELA**

N South America. *Area:* 352,143 sq. mi. (more than twice the size of California). *Pop.:* | 14,529,000. *Cap.:* Caracas. *Off. Lang.:* Spanish. *Money:* 100 centimos = 1 bolivar.

1925–26   1940   1947–48

1956–57   1975

VIET NAM

SE Asia. *Area:* 126,436 sq. mi. (the size of New Mexico). *Pop.:* 52,127,000. *Cap.:* Hanoi. *Lang.:* Vietnamese. *Money:* 10 francs = 1 piaster.

1951

1951

1954

1956

1957

1958–59

1958–59

1959

1968

1968

1971

YEMEN ARAB REPUBLIC

S Arabian Peninsula. *Area:* 75,290 sq. mi. (slightly smaller than South Dakota). *Pop.:* 5,126,000. *Cap.:* Sana. *Lang.:* Arabic. *Money:* 40 bugshas = 1 imadi; since 1962, 40 bugshas = 1 riyal.

1940

1940

1964

1974

Extra Pages for Special Stamps

Extra Pages for Special Stamps

Extra Pages for Special Stamps